JUSTICE AND DIPLOMACY

Diplomacy is used primarily to advance the interests of a state beyond its borders, within a set of global norms intended to assure a degree of international harmony. As a result of internal and international armed conflicts, the need to negotiate peace through an emerging system of international humanitarian and criminal law has required nations to use diplomacy to negotiate "peace versus justice" trade-offs. *Justice and Diplomacy* is the product of a research project conducted by the International Bar Association and the Académie Diplomatique Internationale and focuses on specific moments of collision or contradiction in diplomatic and judicial processes during the humanitarian crises in Bosnia, Rwanda, Kosovo, Darfur, and Libya. The five case studies present critical issues at the intersection of justice and diplomacy, including the role of timing, signaling, legal terminology, accountability, and compliance. Each case study focuses on a specific moment and dynamic, highlighting the key issues and lessons learned.

Mark S. Ellis is Executive Director of the International Bar Association, and the former legal advisor to the Independent International Commission on Kosovo.

Yves Doutriaux is a member of the French Conseil d'État, and a former Ambassador and spokesperson for the French Foreign Ministry.

Timothy W. Ryback is former Deputy Director-General of the Académie Diplomatique Internationale in Paris and Director of the Institute for Historical Justice and Reconciliation.

Justice and Diplomacy

RESOLVING CONTRADICTIONS IN DIPLOMATIC
PRACTICE AND INTERNATIONAL HUMANITARIAN LAW

Edited by

MARK S. ELLIS
YVES DOUTRIAUX
TIMOTHY W. RYBACK

CAMBRIDGE
UNIVERSITY PRESS

CAMBRIDGE
UNIVERSITY PRESS

University Printing House, Cambridge CB2 8BS, United Kingdom

One Liberty Plaza, 20th Floor, New York, NY 10006, USA

477 Williamstown Road, Port Melbourne, VIC 3207, Australia

314–321, 3rd Floor, Plot 3, Splendor Forum, Jasola District Centre,
New Delhi – 110025, India

79 Anson Road, #06–04/06, Singapore 079906

Cambridge University Press is part of the University of Cambridge.

It furthers the University's mission by disseminating knowledge in the pursuit of
education, learning, and research at the highest international levels of excellence.

www.cambridge.org
Information on this title: www.cambridge.org/9781316510889
DOI: 10.1017/9781108624459

© Cambridge University Press 2018

First published 2018

Printed in the United States of America by Sheridan Books, Inc.

A *catalogue record for this publication is available from the British Library.*

Library of Congress Cataloging-in-Publication Data
NAMES: Doutriaux, Yves, editor. | Ellis, Mark S., editor. | Ryback, Timothy W., editor.
TITLE: Justice and diplomacy : resolving contradictions in diplomatic practice and
international humanitarian law / edited by Yves Doutriaux, University of Paris; Mark Ellis,
International Bar Association; Timothy W. Ryback, Academie Diplomatique Internationale.
DESCRIPTION: Cambridge, United Kingdom ; New York, NY, USA : Cambridge University
Press, 2018. | Includes index.
IDENTIFIERS: LCCN 2017043872 | ISBN 9781316510889
SUBJECTS: LCSH: Humanitarian intervention. | Humanitarian law. | International criminal
law. | Diplomacy.
CLASSIFICATION: LCC KZ6369 .J875 2018 | DDC 341.3/3–dc23
LC record available at https://lccn.loc.gov/2017043872

ISBN 978-1-316-51088-9 Hardback
ISBN 978-1-108-44171-1 Paperback

Contents

Editors, Task Force Members, and Researchers

This project has been made possible through the generous support of the International Bar Association and the Federal Department of Foreign Affairs of Switzerland.

Editors
Mark S. Ellis
Yves Doutriaux
Timothy W. Ryback

Task Force Members
Yves Doutriaux *(Co-Chair)*
Mark S. Ellis *(Co-Chair)*
Hans Corell
Alvaro De Soto
Richard J. Goldstone
Diane Orentlicher
Hisashi Owada
Jacques Rupnik
Timothy W. Ryback
David J. Scheffer

Task Force and Researchers Coordinator
Gabriella Lazzoni

Principal Researchers
Marco Bocchese
Agnieska Fall
Mark Kersten
Ari Shaw
Kristina Velcikova

Additional Researchers

Additional research was provided by the following scholars and students principally from Harvard University, the University of Oxford and the Paris Institute of Political Studies (SciencesPo):

Ilina Angelova
Marie Becker
Charles Bishop
Lorenza Cocco
Linda Eggert
Megan Grazier
Elizabeth Horton
Patrick Jones
Lauren Kang
Pali Kata
Laura Lazzoni
Joan Lopez
Kristine Lunde-Tellefsen
Daniel Montoya
Anahita Namaki
Carine Placzek
Ricardo Santos
Delany Sisiruca
Devony Schmidt
Nicholas Tan
Erika Veidis
Lisa Whiler
Michael Wislocki

The opinions expressed in these case studies do not necessarily reflect those of the individual contributors or supporting institutions.

Preface

Justice and Diplomacy is designed for diplomats and jurists engaged in peace negotiations in conflict regions, countries undergoing political transitions following mass atrocities, and other international situations involving suspected war crimes, crimes against humanity, genocide, or other serious violations of international law.

The volume is divided into five case studies, each presenting a critical issue at the intersection of diplomatic and judicial processes, including the role of timing, signaling, legal terminology, and compliance. The Conclusion presents reflections on the relationship between law and diplomacy and reviews "lessons learned" for avoiding contradictions between diplomatic and judicial processes in cases involving international humanitarian and international criminal law.

The parameters for this project were initially framed at a two-day meeting of eminent jurists and diplomats, at the Académie Diplomatique Internationale in Paris, in June 2012. Research and writing of the case studies were coordinated by the Académie Diplomatique Internationale and the International Bar Association, under the auspices of an international Task Force, with funding from the Swiss Federal Department of Foreign Affairs and the International Bar Association, and research support from SciencesPo in France, Harvard University in the United States, and the University of Oxford in the United Kingdom. The International Task Force meetings were convened at the Conseil d'État in Paris, and at All Souls College in Oxford.

The project also benefited from the time and expertise of numerous individuals, including Prince Zeid Ra'ad Al-Hussein, Prof. David Michael Crane, Prof. Talbot D'Alemberte, Stuart Alford, James Goldston, Jerome de Hemptinne, Tim Hughes, Natasha Kandič, Mary McGowan Davis, Prof. Michael Newton, Peter Penford, Antonia Pereira de Sousa, Michael Reynolds, Prof. Michael Scharf, John Shattuck, Jamie Shea, David Tolbert, and Lord Michael Williams of Baglan. Particular appreciation is due to the members of the Task Force.

Introduction

In July 2011, Britain's Foreign Secretary offered some well-meaning but misleading counsel for Muammar Gaddafi. At a press conference in London, William Hague suggested several courses of action for the Libyan president who had been indicted by the International Criminal Court for war crimes and crimes against humanity as a result of his brutal response to emerging insurrection in his country.[1] Hague suggested Gaddafi had two options: he could relinquish power and retire with impunity in Libya or an alternate safe-haven country, or he could face prosecution by the International Criminal Court in The Hague.

When asked by a reporter if the offer of impunity contravened the indictment issued by the International Criminal Court (ICC) prosecutor, the British Foreign Secretary answered firmly but vaguely, "I think you are trying to take us down a hypothetical route." For the prosecutor's office, there was nothing hypothetical about the Libyan president's criminal status. Responding on behalf of ICC prosecutor Luis Moreno-Ocampo, a spokesperson from his office observed that the indictment was a "legal fact" not an option. Under international law there was only one course of action regarding Libya's president: "He has to be arrested."

The British position was particularly vexing for the Court. The United Kingdom had been among the first states to sign and ratify the Rome Statute of the International Criminal Court, which obligated member states to "cooperate fully with the Court in its investigation and prosecution of crimes." William Hague's offer of prospective immunity to Gaddafi, with its implication that the Court's indictments were non-definitive, contravened provisions for cooperation with the Court, particularly in the realms of investigation, prosecution, and compliance that included Article 89 of the Statute requiring the arrest and surrender of indictees, and Article 93 requiring full support in the investigation. If a state fails to cooperate and thereby interferes with the execution of the legal process, "the Court may make

---

[1] M. S. Ellis, "Peace for All or Justice for One?" *The New York Times*, August 11, 2011.

a finding to that effect and refer the matter to the Assembly of States Parties or [. . .] the Security Council," of which the United Kingdom is one of the five permanent members.

William Hague's offer of prospective immunity also appeared to run counter to Britain's voting record as a permanent member of the United Nation's Security Council. In February 2011, Britain voted for United Nations Security Council (UNSC) Resolution 1970, unanimously adopted by the fifteen-member body, referring the situation in Libya to the ICC prosecutor. One month later, Britain also supported UNSC Resolution 1973 that restated the Security Council's February referral to the ICC prosecutor and stressed "that those responsible for or complicit in attacks targeting the civilian population, including aerial and naval attacks, must be held to account." Britain's representative on the Security Council, Mark Lyall Grant, pledged that partners in the North Atlantic Treaty Organization (NATO) and the Arab League "were now ready to act to support the text."[2]

As a party to the Rome Statute, Great Britain had legally bound itself to cooperate with the ICC. As a member of the UN Security Council, it had twice voted for resolutions calling for the investigation that led to Gaddafi's indictments and arrest warrant. And yet, four months after the second vote, the British Foreign Secretary appeared to contravene these obligations by offering Gaddafi the option of safe haven from prosecution. The capture and killing of Gaddafi by opposition militia outside the coastal Libyan town of Sirte in October 2011 resolved the issue, but the public contretemps between the British Foreign Secretary and the ICC prosecutor's office highlighted the contradictions and complexities between the traditional practice of diplomacy – compromise and negotiation – and the less flexible parameters imposed by the emerging system of international humanitarian law.

Hague's position is not surprising from an historical perspective. There was a time when states were the only relevant actors within international law. Given distinctions of politics, culture, religion, and history, and the uncompromising nature of state sovereignty, it was impossible to apply a uniform set of rules at the international level except as a matter of state action and diplomatic effort. However, over the last half century there has been a shift away from the accepted doctrine that international law was the exclusive domain of the sovereign state.[3] Today, the interpretation of international law has expanded to include and recognize new actors as entities of legitimate concern. Nowhere has this been more relevant than in the sphere of international criminal and human rights law, where the preeminent focus is on the individual, even with the borders of sovereign states.

[2] "Security Council Approves 'No-Fly Zone' over Libya, Authorizing 'All Necessary Measures' to Protect Civilians, by Vote of 10 in Favour with 5 Abstentions," United Nations Press Coverage, March 17, 2011.
[3] See M. S. Ellis, "Combating Impunity and Enforcing Accountability as a Way to Promote Peace and Stability – The Role of International War Crimes Tribunals" (2006) 2 *Journal of National Security Law & Policy*, 1.

Modern international law now extends beyond the regulation of interstate conduct, and into regulation of the conduct between the state and the individual. A new doctrine – that individual human rights might, under certain conditions, take precedence over state sovereignty – changed the international legal order forever. One part of this emergent human rights doctrine is particularly relevant. The crime of genocide (according to the 1948 Genocide Convention[4]), crimes against humanity (as defined by the Nuremberg Charter[5]), grave breaches (as set out in the four Geneva Conventions of 1949[6] and their two Additional Protocols[7]), and torture (as defined in the 1984 Convention Against Torture[8]) have all been recognized as grave violations of international law. And with this new doctrine has come recognition that governments' power to grant impunity for these crimes should be limited.

The accountability mechanism for gross violations of human rights and mass atrocities is a relatively recent development. After World War II, the international military tribunals in Nuremberg and Tokyo established a preliminary practice of legal actions against the main perpetrators of such crimes, but the Cold War led to the suspension of the international fight for accountability for more than four decades. It was only after the end of the Cold War and the horrors witnessed in Cambodia, Rwanda and in the former Yugoslavia that international justice returned to the spotlight, resulting in an acceleration of the development of international human rights law and accountability mechanisms. But even this process was slow and dependent on negotiation and consensus among sovereign states.

It was not until May 25, 1993, two years after the beginning of violence in Slovenia, that the United Nations Security Council passed Resolution 827, establishing the International Criminal Tribunal for the former Yugoslavia (ICTY). It took more than six months following the start of the genocide in Rwanda, in April 1994, for the United Nations Security Council to adopt Resolution 955, in November 1994, establishing the International Criminal Tribunal for Rwanda. The case of

---

[4] Convention on the Prevention and Punishment of the Crime of Genocide, Paris, December 9, 1948, in force January 12, 1951, 78 UNTS 277, Art. 1.

[5] Charter of the International Military Tribunal, London, August 8, 1945, 82 UNTC 280, Art. 6(c).

[6] Convention (No. I) for the Amelioration of the Condition of the Wounded and Sick in Armed Forces in the Field, Geneva, August 12, 1949, in force October 21, 1950, 75 UNTS 31; Convention (No. II) for the Amelioration of the Condition of Wounded, Sick and Shipwrecked Members of Armed Forces at Sea, Geneva, August 12, 1949, in force October 21, 1950, 75 UNTS 85; Convention (No. III) Relative to the Treatment of Prisoners of War, Geneva, August 12, 1949, in force October 21, 1950, 75 UNTS 135; Convention (No. IV) Relative to the Protection of Civilian Persons in Time of War, Geneva, August 12, 1949, in force October 21, 1950, 75 UNTS 287.

[7] Protocol Additional to the Geneva Conventions of August 12, 1949, and relating to the Protection of Victims of International Armed Conflicts (Protocol I), Geneva, June 8, 1977, in force December 7, 1978, 1125 UNTS 3; Protocol Additional to the Geneva Conventions of August 12, 1949, and relating to the Protection of Victims of Non-International Armed Conflicts (Protocol II), Geneva, June 8, 1977, in force December 7, 1978, 1125 UNTS 609.

[8] Convention Against Torture and Other Cruel, Inhuman or Degrading Treatment or Punishment, New York, December 10, 1984, in force June 26, 1987, 1465 UNTS 85.

Cambodia is perhaps the most extreme example. It was only in April 2005 that an agreement between the United Nations and the government of Cambodia, which established a UN-sponsored tribunal within the Cambodian legal system, entered into force. The first indictment was issued in 2008, twenty-nine years after the fall of the Khmer Rouge regime in 1979. Oftentimes these tribunals take on a life of their own with dynamics unanticipated by their creators,[9] resulting in ever more complicated relations between the world of diplomacy and international justice.

The ICC, established in 2002 by the Rome Statute, was intended to replace the complex political process of ad hoc tribunals and to provide a permanent international mechanism for the prosecution of individuals for war crimes, genocide, crimes against humanity, and aggression. The ICC was a milestone development in international law. The notion that "crimes against international law are committed by men, not by abstract entities"[10] became the central pillar of international criminal law. And so did the responsibility to hold these individuals to account. Whereas states could grant amnesty or pardon individuals charged with violating national criminal law, that power would not extend to absolving gross human rights violations. Enforcing accountability over impunity became a hallmark of international law.

Still, the interplay between law and diplomacy is complex. It was never anticipated that accountability mechanisms like war crimes tribunals would be called upon to act in the midst of ongoing conflicts. Modeled after the post-World War II Nuremberg Tribunal, there was a presumption that justice was part of an accountability and reparations process, not something concurrent with continuing hostilities and diplomatic efforts to end them. However, the reality of multi-year conflicts in the post-World War II world created a "law and diplomacy equation" in which accountability has become part of the process of "unwinding the conflict."

The reach of international humanitarian justice has expanded significantly in recent decades, and although the principles and dynamics underlying judicial and diplomatic processes have remained essentially unchanged, judicial and political institutions are clearly and fundamentally different. International courts and tribunals are designed to function independently and render impartial justice. International institutions like the United Nations Security Council are designed to maintain peace and are necessarily political. When you have judicial and political institutions involved in the same situation, there is significant potential for confusion and contradictions.

It should be noted that this book does not address in detail the peace versus justice debate, which has been extensively explored. Instead, these case studies provide an examination of those moments in international crises where parallel diplomatic and judicial processes meet and occasionally collide. The purpose is to permit diplomats

---

[9]   Note for instance that the death penalty in Rwanda was abolished as a result of the Rwanda Tribunal.
[10] Nuremberg International Military Tribunal, "Judgment" (1974) reprinted in 41 AJIL, 172, pp. 221–223.

and jurists alike to derive insights and lessons that can better inform future decision-making processes.

CASE STUDIES

The case studies in this volume highlight several critical issues that diplomats and jurists have confronted at the intersection between diplomatic and judicial processes. These include the impact – positive and negative – of timing and signaling both in judicial and diplomatic processes; understanding the practical implications for states in the use of legal terminology, such as the terms genocide, war crimes and crimes against humanity; and the obligations for cooperation and compliance with accountability mechanisms under existing international law.

Each case study focuses on a particular issue, detailing the diplomatic and judicial processes, identifying points of contradiction, examining "lessons learned," and outlining parameters for action within the framework of international law. Each case is clearly unique, with its own complexities of actors and imperatives, and although the lessons may or may not be applicable to a specific case in the future, it is the hope of the editors that fresh insights can be derived for both diplomats and jurists in facing such situations.

The case of *Bosnia* reviews the impact of criminal indictments on diplomatic negotiations to end the war in Bosnia and Herzegovina and raises the question whether legal accountability can be developed as a more effective tool in diplomatic negotiating strategies. The *Rwanda* case was chosen as an example where confusion about legal terminology among diplomats caused procrastination in taking timely action in responding to the genocide occurring in Rwanda in 1994. In the *Kosovo* study, the complex diplomatic and judicial processes involved in executing an international arrest warrant for sitting and former high-level government officials is examined. More specifically, it illustrates the challenges facing diplomats in negotiating with indicted heads of state, and the political and diplomatic mechanisms through which cooperation with international tribunals can nevertheless be encouraged or enforced. In regard to *Darfur*, the first instance where the United Nations Security Council passed a resolution referring a potential case of genocide by the head of state to the International Criminal Court, the problem of timing and signaling between judicial and diplomatic efforts in pursuit of the respective goals of justice is discussed. In particular, this case study analyzes the signals resulting from contradictory actions of diplomats trying to end decades of regional conflict in Sudan and the UNSC referring the situation to the ICC as a response to the findings of an International Commission of Inquiry alleging that genocide was occurring. The *Libya* study reveals the difficult tension between peace and justice and underscores the need for diplomats to understand the full implications of a Security Council referral to the ICC.

Understanding and appreciating the fragile, yet potentially beneficial relationship between law and diplomacy is the core thesis of this book. Diplomats and jurists alike must be informed about the international justice system and the delicate web of political acts and contingencies upon which it rests. It is also imperative that the international community treats the contradictions, complications and failures of the past as lessons for the future.

1

Accountability

Diplomatic Negotiation and Judicial Process

FOCUS: BOSNIA

Executive summary: This case study examines the impact of criminal indictments on diplomatic negotiations to end the war in Bosnia and Herzegovina. On July 24, 1995, the Chief Prosecutor of the International Criminal Tribunal for the former Yugoslavia (ICTY) indicted Bosnian Serb President Radovan Karadžić and Serbian military leader Ratko Mladić on sixteen counts of grave breaches of the laws or customs of war, crimes against humanity, and genocide. On November 16, 1995, an additional twenty counts of war crimes and crimes against humanity were added to the indictments, as well as two counts of genocide for "the summary executions of Bosnian Muslim men and women" pertaining to the massacre at Srebrenica. Both indictees – key actors in the conflict – were excluded from participating in the November 1995 negotiations at Wright-Patterson Air Force Base near Dayton, Ohio, which resulted in the General Framework Agreement for Peace in Bosnia and Herzegovina to end the Yugoslav wars. In so doing, the indictments, initially seen as an obstruction to the diplomatic process, bolstered a US-led strategy to isolate the Bosnian Serbs and to negotiate with Slobodan Milošević, president of Republic of Serbia, as the exclusive representative of the Serb delegation to the talks.

The case study illustrates how a judicial act – indictments that initially appeared to complicate diplomatic efforts to resolve the Bosnian conflict – was exploited to diplomatic advantage at the negotiating table. The case raises the following questions: Can judicial and diplomatic processes be aligned in order to meet the imperatives of both international law and conflict resolution? Can such alignment occur by design or simply by coincidence? Can legal accountability be developed as a more effective tool in diplomatic negotiating strategies without politicizing judicial processes, which could undermine the legitimacy of international tribunals? The case study underscores how diplomatic efforts that harness accountability mechanisms, such as indictments, can bolster the aims of conflict resolution by sidelining potential spoilers.

1.1 INTRODUCTION

The ICTY was created in the midst of ongoing conflicts between Bosnian Muslims, Serbs, and Croats. International pressure, galvanized by media reports depicting grave human rights abuses, from ethnic cleansing to genocide, sparked calls for intervention to end the violence. This case study examines the relationship between dual processes of intervention: judicial intervention by the ICTY, and diplomatic/military intervention by the USA and its NATO allies. Specifically, it centers on the indictment of Serb officials Radovan Karadžić and Ratko Mladić by the ICTY, and the impact of accountability mechanisms on efforts to resolve the Yugoslav wars.

1.2 ESTABLISHING THE ICTY AND EARLY WESTERN ENGAGEMENT

The ICTY was a unique institution in the sense that it was created by the UN Security Council to prosecute violations of humanitarian law in the territory of the former Yugoslavia while the conflict in the territory was still *ongoing*.[1] Established on May 25, 1993, the Tribunal's function was not simply to prosecute perpetrators of international crimes but also to "contribute to the restoration and maintenance of peace."[2] Advocates employed the language of "justice in real time" to suggest the Tribunal could take an active role in deterring further violence through criminal accountability.[3]

The ICTY represented the first time the UN Security Council used its authority under Chapter VII of the UN Charter to create a tribunal. Despite bearing the imprimatur of the Security Council, the lofty ambitions for the ICTY were not initially met with sufficient support to create effective mechanisms of enforcement. It took over a year for the Tribunal to gain enough staff and resources to function.[4] Yet, as the conflict raged and political pressure grew for some form of intervention, more investigators and funding were deployed, particularly from the USA, and South African Judge Richard Goldstone took the helm as Chief Prosecutor.

The Tribunal began its work by indicting low-ranking criminals.[5] In November 1994, Dragan Nikolić, a minor official known as "Jenki," was indicted for his role as commander of the Serb-run Sušica Detention Camp in the municipality of Vlasenica. However, the Tribunal had only held a Rule 61[6] hearing in which evidence against the accused had been publicly aired. The first official trial

[1] Security Council Res. 808 (February 22, 1993), UN Doc. S/RES/808.
[2] Security Council Res. 827 (May 25, 1993), UN Doc. S/RES/827.
[3] L. Vinjamuri, "Case Study: Justice, Peace and Deterrence in the Former Yugoslavia" (November 2013), European Council on Foreign Relations, p. 2.
[4] J. R. McAllister, "On Knife's Edge: The International Criminal Tribunal for the Former Yugoslavia's Impact on Violence Against Civilians," PhD thesis, Northwestern University (2014), pp. 79–80.
[5] M. Schrag, "Lessons Learned from ICTY Experience" (2004) 2 *Oxford Journal of International Criminal Justice*, 2, pp. 427–433.
[6] Rules of Procedure and Evidence, February 11, 1994, as amended July 24, 2009, ICTY IT/32/Rev. 43, Rule 61.

before the ICTY was for Duško Tadić, a former bar owner and president of a local Serb Democratic Party board in the small town of Kozerać. Such minor achievements revealed the challenges facing ICTY investigators. The Office of the Prosecutor met resistance from both regional and international officials, and it struggled to gather evidence and share information with allied organizations.[7]

Despite the absence of a unified strategy to align diplomatic and judicial efforts, Western officials – particularly US policy makers – were closely intertwined with the creation and institutional development of the ICTY. Western involvement in the conflict in the former Yugoslavia was generally uncoordinated in the aftermath of the Cold War.[8] The United States, for its part, remained largely disengaged in the early years of the war, hoping European nations would find a resolution and preempt any need for US involvement in a regional conflict. But as a European-led resolution seemed increasingly untenable, an intensified US initiative to end the conflict also spurred increasing activity at the ICTY.[9] ICTY Chief Prosecutor Richard Goldstone recalled being "warmly welcomed by Madeleine Albright, who had played a leading role in having the tribunal established."[10] He also observed that Albright appointed David Scheffer "to take special responsibility for moving the work of the tribunal forward."[11]

The nature of Western engagement in the region, along with existing links between key stakeholders, set the background against which both the ICTY indictments and the Dayton process unfolded. This context is important for understanding how US officials leveraged the indictments in pursuing a peace accord. The US role in, and commitment to, the creation and effective functioning of the ICTY presaged a willingness to seize upon the coincidental yet complementary indictments to facilitate a diplomatic resolution.

1.3 THE INDICTMENTS OF KARADŽIĆ AND MLADIĆ

On July 25, 1995, the ICTY succeeded in indicting Bosnian Serb leaders Ratko Mladić and Radovan Karadžić on sixteen counts of genocide, crimes against humanity, and war crimes.[12] The first formal indictment proceedings against Mladić and Karadžić had begun as early as the spring of 1995. In April, the OTP

---

7 McAllister, "On Knife's Edge," pp. 82–83.

8 For an analysis of Western involvement in the Yugoslav conflict, see J. Glaudric, *The Hour of Europe: Western Powers and the Breakup of Yugoslavia* (New Haven: Yale University Press, 2011), p. 8.

9 The US involvement will be discussed in more detail below. For an account of the intensifying strife to achieve peace in Bosnia within the US Administration, see D. Chollet and B. Freeman, *The Secret History of Dayton: US Diplomacy and the Bosnia Peace Process 1995* (National Security Archive Electronic Briefing Book No. 171, 2005), especially chapter 1.

10 R. Goldstone, *For Humanity: Reflections of a War Crimes Investigator* (New Haven: Yale University Press, 2000), p. 78.

11 Ibid.

12 M. Fiori, "The Indictment against Radovan Karadžić: An Analysis of the Legal Developments in the ICTY's Crucial Upcoming Trial" (2008) 3 *The Hague Justice Journal*, 6.

publicly requested that Bosnian authorities defer their investigations of Mladić and Karadžić to the jurisdiction of the ICTY given the scope of crimes at issue.[13] The first indictment accused Mladić and Karadžić of perpetrating genocide, crimes against humanity, and other violations tied to the sniper campaign in Sarajevo. It also accused the Serbian leaders of abetting the seizure and use of 284 UN peacekeepers as human shields.[14]

Two weeks earlier, on July 11, nearly 25,000 Bosnian Muslims began to flee escalating violence in the eastern town of Srebrenica. Serb forces intercepted the refugees, separating men and boys from women, children, and the elderly. Over the following days, Serb forces summarily executed between 7,000 and 8,000 civilians, predominantly Bosnian Muslim males.[15] On November 16, 1995, the OTP issued a second indictment against Mladić and Karadžić, adding new charges of war crimes, crimes against humanity, and genocide to reflect the egregious violations of international humanitarian law during the Srebrenica massacre.[16]

This indictment was not intentionally timed to coincide with diplomatic processes. Indeed, Goldstone acknowledged that the announcement of the Dayton process hastened the indictment, but the precise timing of indictment remained coincidental.[17]

As discussed in more detail below, the indictments marginalized Karadžić and Mladić from the Dayton talks, thereby bolstering the US strategy to negotiate exclusively with Milošević. The following section will look at the development of diplomatic relations in the preparatory phase of the Dayton Peace Talks and the nature of the relationship between Western diplomats and the Bosnian Serb leadership. In particular, it will focus on the months between the first indictment and the beginning of the talks, highlighting the coincidental timing of the indictment and the *strategic* decision by US diplomats to use the indictments to facilitate diplomatic objectives.

1.4 MARGINALIZING MLADIĆ AND KARADŽIĆ

The Dayton Peace Talks followed two failed attempts at brokering peace in Bosnia and Herzegovina: the Carrington-Cutileiro plan, rejected in 1992 by the Bosnian-Muslim leader Alija Izetbegović, and the Vance-Owen plan, rejected in 1993 by the Bosnian Serbs. The Dayton Peace Talks were premised on the three basic assumptions, or "pillars," for peace, formulated by the Contact Group comprised of the

---

[13] "The Judges Will Soon Consider Two Applications for Deferral in Matters Related to Bosnian Croats and the Bosnian Serb Leadership," International Criminal Tribunal for the Former Yugoslavia Press Release, April 24, 1995.

[14] McAllister, "On Knife's Edge," p. 112.

[15] Ibid., p. 107. See also S. Power, *A Problem from Hell: America and the Age of Genocide* (New York: Basic Books, 2002).

[16] McAllister, "On Knife's Edge."   [17] Goldstone, *For Humanity*, p. 229.

United States, Russia, Britain, France, and Germany: (1) Bosnia would remain a single state; (2) this state would consist of a Federation and a Bosnian Serb entity; and (3) these two entities would be linked by a set of mutually agreed constitutional principles. These basic principles were accepted by all actors, although Bosnian Serb leaders were reluctant to do so. A 51–49 territorial division between the Bosniaks (Bosnian Muslims) and the Bosnian Serbs was also accepted by the Bosnian and Serb governments (represented by Izetbegović and Milošević, respectively). However, this was a tenuous agreement in principle that raised strong objections among other members of the Serbian leadership.

The recalcitrant Serb leadership proved an impediment to peace negotiations from the outset. In the months leading up to the November 2005 talks in Dayton, continuing hostilities between Bosnian Serbs and Bosniaks, and the siege of Sarajevo (April 5, 1992, to February 26, 1996) in particular, compelled further engagement by the United States and NATO allies. The Clinton Administration, for which "Bosnia seemed to overshadow its entire foreign policy,"[18] pushed for an ultimatum to the Bosnian Serb leadership, threatening NATO bombing if Serb-led violence did not cease. In response to the threat of NATO airstrikes, Mladić took a firm stand, invoking "Balkan history, culture and politics" and ardently claiming that "Serbs were doing nothing more than fighting for their own territory."[19] Clinton later recalled that "diplomacy could not succeed until the Serbs sustained some serious losses on the ground," given the absence of sufficient incentives to come to the negotiating table.[20]

The relationship between the US diplomats and the Bosnian Serb leaders grew increasingly fraught. The launch of the NATO air strikes in August 1995 provided leverage over Bosnian Serbs, but the "lack of political-military coordination" raised concerns that any political advantages of the bombing would quickly wane.[21] For example, in the meetings to discuss Bosnian Serb withdrawal and weapon removal from around Sarajevo, Mladić (despite having been indicted by the ICTY, and despite the ongoing NATO bombing) was "unrepentant and bullish as ever [and] threatened to unleash all of the BSA [Bosnian Serb Army] forces against the remaining enclaves."[22] Put simply, Mladić and Karadžić were clear impediments to peace negotiations and had to be marginalized. However, the lack of coordination between military and diplomatic strategies rendered such efforts more difficult to pursue.

[18] This quote and subsequent quotations are taken from a declassified 1997 US State Department study of the American effort to end the Bosnian war. In further citations, the study will be referred to as "Declassified Study." For more information on the study, see D. Chollet and B. Freeman, *The Secret History of Dayton*.

[19] D. Chollet, "Through the Window of Opportunity: The Endgame Strategy" in D. Chollet, *The Road to the Dayton Accords* (Springer, 2007), p. 25.

[20] B. Clinton, *My Life* (New York: Knopf, 2004), p. 667.

[21] D. Chollet, "Force and Diplomacy: NATO Bombing Ends, the Western Offensive Heats Up," in D. Chollet, *The Road to the Dayton Accords* (Springer, 2007), p. 100. See also R. Holbrooke, *To End a War* (New York: Modern Library Inc, 1999), p. 145.

[22] Chollet, "Force and Diplomacy," p. 101.

1.5 TIMING OF THE INDICTMENTS

As to the extent to which the indictments had an impact on peace negotiations, it is important to examine the timing and context within which they were issued. Some observers have argued that the Tribunal's early emphasis on low-level officials was a prosecutorial choice stemming from "insufficient appreciation of political issues and perceptions," that is, a lack of coordination between political and judicial actors.[23] However, this presumes that such formal coordination is a desirable and feasible strategic choice. For Goldstone, the first indictment against the low-level official Nikolić was necessary to demonstrate that the ICTY was working and thus worthy of continued financial support.[24] In the absence of cooperation with the Tribunal, the Nikolić case was the only one with enough evidence to warrant an indictment. Goldstone also underscored that "the process of issuing an indictment is highly complex," contingent upon evidence gathering and judicial chamber review, among other factors. The propitious timing of an indictment with favorable political circumstances is therefore "a coincidence."[25] In the case of Karadžić and Mladić, sufficient evidence was not available.

The lack of formal coordination between diplomatic and judicial processes should not be understood to mean that external developments went unnoticed by the OTP in timing the indictments of Karadžić and Mladić. To be sure, the OTP was an independent body distinct from the realpolitik of the Security Council. Goldstone underscored that there was no direct political pressure on him to indict Karadžić and Mladić. In fact, Secretary-General Boutros-Ghali "made it clear that had [Goldstone] consulted him, he would have advised [him] not to indict Karadžić before peace had been brokered in Bosnia."[26]

Nonetheless, there are several accounts suggesting that external circumstances did affect the decision-making process about issuing the indictments of Karadžić and Mladić at this particular juncture. Goldstone recalls developing friendly relationships with the Croatian and Bosnian government, in particular with Ivan Simonović, the Croatian Deputy Minister of Foreign Affairs and Muhamad Sacirbey, Bosnia's permanent representative to the UN (who then became the Foreign Minister). Such collegiality did not exist with Serbian authorities because of the "extreme antagonism toward, and suspicion of, the tribunal on the Serb side."[27] Thus, collecting evidence against Karadžić and Mladić was easier than collecting evidence against Milošević, contributing to their indictment at an earlier point.

Goldstone also noted that the Karadžić and Mladić cases were prioritized because of "persistent stories of the massacre of thousands of Muslim men and boys by the Bosnian Serb Army, led by Mladić."[28] The crimes committed by the Bosnian Serbs were discussed at the UN and occupied a prominent place on the international

---

[23] Ibid.   [24] Goldstone, *For Humanity*, p. 105.   [25] Ibid., p. 108.   [26] Ibid., p. 103.
[27] Ibid., p. 99.   [28] Ibid., p. 108.

political agenda. In the months preceding the indictment, representatives of Bosnian Muslims (and the Bosnian government) – Mr. Misić and Mr. Sacirbey – were present at the Security Council meetings on June 23, July 5, and July 12, 1995. They took seats at the invitation of the Council's President, in accordance with Rule 37 of the provisional rules of procedure. The Security Council provided a forum for the Bosnian government to air its grievances and to increase international pressure on the Serbs. On June 23, 1995, the Security Council stated that it was "deeply concerned at . . . the obstruction by the Bosnian Serb party of freedom of movement and utilities and the continued obstruction of the normal operation of Sarajevo airport."[29] On July 5, while discussing the destruction caused by Bosnian Serbs, Mr. Sacirbey from Bosnia-Herzegovina went a step further, and referred to them as "Karadžić Serbs."[30] This language was used again by Mr. Misić on July 12 when, in referring to the events in Srebrenica, he stated that "Karadžić's hordes had 'ethnically cleansed' [a Bosnian village] at the beginning of the war . . . . To those familiar with the Karadžić methods, it was clear even then that Srebrenica had yet to experience its moment of greatest despair."[31] In the same meeting, Mr. Merimee from France stated that "we had faced incessant violations of the status of the safe areas, but we had not yet had to confront a deliberate intention on the part of the Bosnian Serbs to use force to occupy a safe area. This is what has just been done by General Mladić's troops."[32]

The above analysis draws attention to two features of these meetings, which may have influenced the timing of indictments of Karadžić and Mladić. First, Karadžić and Mladić are explicitly and directly linked to the atrocities taking place in Bosnia and Herzegovina. Second, the involvement of Serbia (as opposed to Bosnian Serbs) is not discussed. The distinction between these two parties was made explicit by the UK delegate on June 23: "Last August, Belgrade authorities took two important steps towards encouraging the emergence of a peaceful settlement in Bosnia . . . The Bosnian Serb leadership, however, have not yet taken this essential step." The "Belgrade authorities" are framed as a potential partner in peace-making, whereas Bosnian Serbs are cast as unwilling to negotiate or cease hostilities. Thus, the international political climate, which had rhetorically indicted the Bosnian Serbs for their role in the conflict, set the backdrop against which ICTY indictments were leveraged to marginalize Mladić and Karadžić from subsequent negotiations.

1.6 LEVERAGING THE INDICTMENTS TO STRENGTHEN THE "MILOŠEVIĆ STRATEGY"

The indictments of Mladić and Karadžić did not immediately result in their exclusion from diplomatic negotiations. To the contrary, US diplomats were

---

[29]　Transcript of Security Council Meeting No. 3548 (June 23, 1995), UN Doc. S/PV.3548.
[30]　Transcript of Security Council Meeting No. 3551 (July 5, 1995), UN Doc. S/PV.3551.
[31]　Transcript of Security Council Meeting No. 3553 (July 12, 1995), UN Doc. S/Pv.3553.　　[32]　Ibid.

uncertain about how the indictments would impact peace negotiations. The Clinton Administration was internally divided over whether and to what extent to support the indictments of Mladić and Karadžić.[33] David Scheffer, Madeleine Albright, and John Shattuck pushed for further cooperation with the ICTY.[34] However, in the face of "fresh evidence of the worst genocide in Europe since World War II,"[35] Mladić and Karadžić were still considered potential negotiation partners, such that a letter from Karadžić to former President Jimmy Carter stating that he welcomed the new US peace initiative was received as "mildly positive" by Administration officials.[36] Moreover, some feared that the advent of the Srebrenica massacre might make it more likely "that European peace negotiators would be tempted to capitulate to the Serbs in a desperate effort to end the crisis at any cost."[37]

In late August, Richard Holbrooke assumed a key role in the peace process. Holbrooke sought to maximize the bargaining position of the US in any subsequent negotiations. As such, he presented US cooperation with the ICTY and therefore enforcement of the indictments as a *fait accompli*.[38] In a discussion of Srebrenica on US television, Holbrooke announced that he was "not going to cut a deal that absolves the people responsible for this."[39] In other words, the US would cooperate with the Tribunal and would not negotiate with any leaders indicted by the ICTY. If Mladić or Karadžić tried to attend any negotiations, Holbrooke remarked, "they'd be arrested and set aside."[40] Both US Secretary of State Warren Christopher and US Ambassador to the UN Madeleine Albright echoed this position and publicly stated that the US would not negotiate with indicted war criminals.

The exclusion of Mladić and Karadžić from negotiations increased diplomats' reliance on the Serbian president, Slobodan Milošević, to "deliver" the Bosnian Serbs. The so-called Milošević Strategy at once elevated Milošević as the person responsible for coalescing Pale (Bosnian Serb) leadership and presented US negotiators with a clear target to ratchet up diplomatic pressure.[41] More specifically, the Milošević Strategy "entailed linking cooperation by Bosnian Serbs to sanctions relief for Milošević, as well as dealing directly with Belgrade, as opposed to Pale, in negotiations."[42] In their account of negotiations, Derek Chollet and Bennett Freeman characterize Milošević as easier to engage than other Bosnian Serb leaders

---

[33] D. Scheffer, *All the Missing Souls: A Personal History of the War Crimes Tribunals* (Princeton: Princeton University Press, 2012), p. 39.

[34] McAllister, "On Knife's Edge," p 119.

[35] J. Shattuck, *Freedom on Fire: Human Rights Wars and America's Response* (Harvard: Harvard University Press, 2005), p. 115.

[36] D. Chollet, "Tragedy as Turning Point: The First Shuttle, Mt. Igman and Operation Deliberate Force," in D. Chollet, *The Road to the Dayton Accords* (Springer, 2007), p. 70.

[37] McAllister, "On Knife's Edge," p. 119.   [38] Ibid., p. 121.   [39] Holbrooke, *To End a War*, p. 90.

[40] McAllister, "On Knife's Edge," p. 121.

[41] D. Chollet, "Endgame: Dayton, November 11–21," in D. Chollet, *The Road to the Dayton Accords* (Springer, 2007), p. 216.

[42] Interview with R. Holbrooke and R. Owen of June 18, 1996, as discussed in McAllister, "On Knife's Edge," p. 121.

due to his manners, language skills, and personality.[43] Holbrooke played off of Milošević's machismo by pitting him against Karadžić and Mladić, encouraging Milošević to overtake the other Serb leaders and demonstrate that he alone spoke for the Bosnian Serbs.[44] Exploiting Milošević's pre-existing ties to the West and Western officials, US negotiators used the possibility of lifting sanctions on Serbia as leverage, and "[Milošević] understood that the bottom line was that he could not leave Dayton without an agreement."[45]

Both the indictments and sustained NATO airstrikes increased pressure on Milošević to cooperate. On August 30, 1995, the Serbian leader handed Holbrooke a letter from the Bosnian Serb leadership and the Patriarch of the Serbian Orthodox church agreeing to form a negotiating team with Milošević as the head. The "Patriarch Paper," as it came to be known, accepted the Contact Group principles as the basis for the negotiations. It reiterated support for the 51–49 territorial division and, furthermore, "suggested that the Bosnian state should be a 'union' within its current boundaries with a Muslim-controlled Sarajevo as its capital."[46] This development not only appeared to solve "the most intractable problem of the negotiations — how to deal with the Bosnian Serbs,"[47] but also signaled Milošević's understanding of the need to reach an agreement and his flexibility on territorial issues. In other words, it seemed to affirm the view that Milošević would be a more credible and willing negotiating partner than Karadžić and Mladić.

To be sure, the ability of Milošević to deliver the entire Serb leadership was never understood to be a foregone conclusion. Several subsequent meetings seemed to raise questions about Milošević's influence over Mladić and Karadžić. For example, at one meeting in September 1995 to negotiate an end to the siege of Sarajevo, Milošević surprised the American delegation in Belgrade by stating that both Mladić and Karadžić were in the compound where the meeting was taking place. Richard Holbrooke and the other members of the US delegation agreed to meet the two men if they satisfied conditions: (1) Milošević must lead the discussion and control them as part of his delegation; and (2) they must be ready for serious discussions and not digress into historical tirades.[48] Milošević agreed, and the two men joined the meeting. Yet, as General Wesley Clark read from a draft proposal to end the siege, Mladić and Karadžić erupted in defiant opposition. Holbrooke rose and, speaking to Milošević, declared: "Mr President, we had an agreement. This behavior is clearly not consistent with it. If your 'friends' . . . do not wish to have a serious discussion, we

[43] D. Chollet, "The Road to Geneva: The Patriarch Letter and NATO Bombing," in D. Chollet, *The Road to the Dayton Accords* (Springer, 2007), p. 75.

[44] McAllister, "On Knife's Edge," p. 124.

[45] D. Chollet, "Opening Talks and Clearing Away the Underbrush: Dayton November 1–10," in D. Chollet, *The Road to the Dayton Accords* (Springer, 2007), p. 185.

[46] D. Chollet, "The Road to Geneva," p. 76.   [47] Ibid.   [48] Holbrooke, *To End a War*, p. 148.

will leave now."[49] Milošević argued with his colleagues and later returned to the US delegation, asking to rejoin the negotiations.

Thus, despite uncertainty about Milošević's capabilities, the Clinton Administration continued to negotiate with Milošević – who proved an able negotiating partner in the lead up to Dayton – on an agreement relating to constitutional principles signed in Geneva; on the ceasefire agreement ending the siege of Sarajevo described above; in New York, where draft principles for subsequent negotiations were agreed upon; and finally in Dayton, where the parties agreed to a framework to end the fighting in Bosnia and Herzegovina.[50] The Milošević Strategy and, more specifically, the marginalization of Karadžić and Mladić from the negotiation process seemed to have the intended result of bolstering the Serb President and consolidating his legitimacy as the lead representative of the Bosnian Serb delegation.

1.7 THE IMPACT OF THE INDICTMENTS ON THE DIPLOMATIC PROCESS

There is agreement among scholars and other observers that the indictment of Karadžić and Mladić facilitated the negotiations of the peace agreement in Dayton (see Orentlicher, Moghalu, Mendez). First, to the extent the indictments by the ICTY facilitated the Milošević Strategy, such judicial action provided valuable leverage for diplomatic efforts to end the war in Bosnia and Herzegovina. US officials made it clear that they would not directly negotiate with indicted war criminals and that Mladić and Karadžić would be arrested if they arrived on US soil. This explicit intent to enforce the actions of the ICTY allowed US officials to exclude the obstinate Mladić and Karadžić as noncredible negotiating partners and thus elevate Milošević as their preferred interlocutor. Milošević had already demonstrated a greater willingness to secure a peace agreement than Mladić and Karadžić. Their removal as potential spoilers enhanced the ability of US negotiators to engage the Serbs through Milošević.

Second, the indictments increased the likelihood that Bosnian leadership would participate in the diplomatic negotiations. The Bosnian–Croatian forces were reluctant to halt military advances, which had been aided by NATO airstrikes against Bosnian Serb positions. Furthermore, any negotiation with Mladić or Karadžić was unacceptable given their widely reported role in the Srebrenica massacre. As Richard Goldstone remarked, "Had [Karadžić] not been indicted, the Dayton Accords would not have been brokered. Karadžić would have been free to attend the meetings, and that would have made the attendance of Alija Izetbegović, the president of Bosnia, impossible."[51] Indeed, Izetbegović and Bosnian Foreign Minister Muhamed Sacirbey had taken a firm stand on the issue of dividing Bosnia or negotiating with war criminals, and they were unwilling to make

---

[49]   Ibid., p. 151.   [50]   McAllister, "On Knife's Edge," p. 127.   [51]   Goldstone, *For Humanity*, p. 103.

concessions. The Milošević Strategy, as enabled by the indictments, offered Holbrooke and the US negotiators a pathway to incentivize Bosnian participation in diplomatic talks. Marginalizing Mladić and Karadžić from the negotiations facilitated the achievement of this pathway.

1.8 CONCLUSION: FUTURE COORDINATION BETWEEN DIPLOMATIC AND JUDICIAL BODIES

This case study illustrates the potential of international criminal indictments to serve the ends of conflict resolution. The indictments of Mladić and Karadžić were issued at a fortuitous moment in the diplomatic efforts to end the war, such that US officials were able and willing to leverage the indictments to exclude spoilers from the Dayton process. This case raises the question of whether diplomatic and judicial efforts can align by design, or whether such outcomes must or should remain coincidental.

This case highlights the interaction of diplomatic and judicial processes particular to the ICTY. While the experiences of the ICTY can elucidate opportunities and challenges for international criminal law more generally, it is important to recognize the institutional differences that might make formal diplomatic and judicial coordination difficult moving forward. For example, the autonomy of the OTP of the International Criminal Court is limited by the role of the pre-trial chamber. Even if the Prosecutor triggers an investigation *proprio motu*, the pre-trial chamber can nonetheless decide that the case is not admissible (Article 18) based on, among other things, insufficient gravity of the case, or the state's jurisdiction over the crime, along with willingness and ability to prosecute (Article 17). This last element is distinct from procedures of the ICTY; whereas the ICTY had supremacy over national courts, the ICC follows the principle of complementarity and can only prosecute if the state with jurisdiction over the crime in question is unwilling or unable to prosecute. The accused, or the state, can also challenge the admissibility of the case at later stages (Article 19). On the other hand, if the Prosecutor refuses to pursue a case triggered by the Security Council or a State Party, they can appeal to the pre-trial chamber and ask it to compel the Prosecutor to pursue the case (Article 53.3). As such, the opportunities for an independent diplomatic advisory to influence prosecutorial decision-making are limited.

Perhaps more importantly, it is not self-evident that diplomatic and judicial actions *should* be coordinated in such a formal, institutionalized manner. Indeed, as Richard Goldstone has noted, the real and perceived independence of the Office of the Prosecutor is the source of its legitimacy and is a requirement for successful investigations and prosecutions.[52] The presence of a formal "diplomatic advisor" to the Prosecutor and/or the Court may undercut its legitimacy by actively politicizing

---

[52] Goldstone, *For Humanity*, p. 88.

decisions about whom to indict (or not indict). In other words, efforts to align diplomatic and judicial actions by design may end up serving neither the ends of conflict resolution nor the ends of justice.

Using accountability to further diplomatic processes is a difficult task that raises many questions as well as practical difficulties. As the case of Karadžić and Mladić demonstrates, international criminal justice can have an impact on the nature of peace processes. However, this relationship should not be overstated. Although accountability mechanisms may *enable* certain outcomes, it is political decisions – such as the US negotiators' decision to insist that persons indicted by the ICTY not participate in the Dayton talks – that capitalize on this potential and ultimately impact diplomacy. Indictment by an international tribunal does not *per se* exclude one from peace negotiations. Prosecutors may be better advised to be individually informed of and sensitive to the larger political and diplomatic context surrounding an investigation, and to how decisions about indictments can impact peace and security.

BIBLIOGRAPHY

Primary Sources

Chollet D. and Freeman B., *The Secret History of Dayton: US Diplomacy and the Bosnia Peace Process* 1995 (National Security Archive Electronic Briefing Book No. 171, 2005).
International Criminal Tribunal for the former Yugoslavia (ICTY) Press Release, *The Judges Will Soon Consider Two Applications for Deferral in Matters Related to Bosnian Croats and the Bosnian Serb Leadership*, April 24, 1995, available at www.icty.org/sid/7246.
Rome Statute of the International Criminal Court, Rome, July 17, 1998, in force July 1, 2002, 2187 UNTS 38544.
Rules of Procedure and Evidence, February 11, 1994, as amended July 24, 2009, ICTY IT/32/ Rev. 43.
Transcript of Security Council Meeting No. 3548 (June 23, 1995), UN Doc. S/PV.3548.
Transcript of Security Council Meeting No. 3551 (July 5, 1995), UN Doc. S/PV.3551.
Transcript of Security Council Meeting No. 3553 (July 12, 1995), UN Doc. S/PV.3553.
United Nations Security Council (UNSC) Res 808 (February 22, 1993), UN Doc. S/Res/808.
UNSC Res 827 (May 25, 1993), UN Doc. S/Res/827.

Secondary Sources

Books
Clinton B., *My Life* (New York: Knopf, 2004).
Daalder I. H., *Getting to Dayton: The Making of America's Bosnia Policy* (Washington, DC: Brookings Institution Press, 2000).
Glaudric J., *The Hour of Europe: Western Powers and the Breakup of Yugoslavia* (New Haven: Yale University Press, 2011).
Goldstone R., *For Humanity: Reflections of a War Crimes Investigator* (New Haven: Yale University Press, 2000).
Holbrooke R., *To End a War* (New York: The Modern Library, 1999).

McAllister J. R., "On Knife's Edge: The International Criminal Tribunal for the Former Yugoslavia's Impact on Violence Against Civilians" PhD thesis, Northwestern University (2014).

Moghalu K. C., *Global Justice: The Politics of War Crimes Trial* (Santa Barbara: Praeger Security International, 2006).

Power S., *A Problem from Hell: America and the Age of Genocide* (New York: Basic Books, 2002).

Scheffer D., *All the Missing Souls: A Personal History of the War Crimes Tribunals* (Princeton: Princeton University Press, 2012).

Shahabuddeen M., *International Criminal Justice at the Yugoslav Tribunal: A Judge's Recollection* (Oxford: Oxford University Press, 2012).

Shattuck J. *Freedom on Fire: Human Rights Wars and America's Response* (Cambridge: Harvard University Press, 2005).

Articles and Reports

Akhavan P., "The Yugoslav Tribunal at a Crossroads: The Dayton Peace Agreement and Beyond" (1996) 18 *Human Rights Quarterly*, 2, pp. 259–285.

Ellis M., "Bringing Justice to an Embattled Region – Creating and Implementing the 'Rules of the Road' for Bosnia-Herzegovina" (1999) 17 *Berkeley Journal of International Law*, 1, pp. 1–25.

Ellis M., Lampe J. R., and Woodward S. L., "Bosnian Economic Security After 1996" (1996) *The Woodrow Wilson International Center for Scholars and The Atlantic Council*.

Fiori M., "The Indictment Against Radovan Karadžić: An Analysis of the Legal Developments in the ICTY's Crucial Upcoming Trial" (2008) 3 *The Hague Justice Journal*, 6.

Gow J., "The ICTY, War Crimes Enforcement and Dayton: The Ghost in the Machine" (2006) 5 *Ethnopolitics*, 1, pp. 49–65.

Holbrooke R., "Richard Holbrooke on the Dayton Peace Accords," *The Daily Beast*, 15 December 2010, available at: www.thedailybeast.com/articles/2010/12/15/richard-holbrooke-on-the-dayton-peace-accords.html.

Mendez J., "The Arrest of Ratko Mladić and its Impact on International Justice and Prevention of Genocide and Other International Crimes," *The Holocaust and United Nations Outreach Programme*, available at: www.un.org/en/holocaustremembrance/docs/pdf/chapter8.pdf.

Orentlicher D. F., "That Someone Guilty Be Punished: The Impact of ICTY in Bosnia" (2010) *Open Society Justice Initiative*.

Schrag M., "Lessons Learned from the ICTY Experience: Notes for the ICC Prosecutor" (2004) 2 *Oxford Journal of International Criminal Justice*, 2, pp. 427–433.

Vinjamuri L., "Case Study: Justice, Peace and Deterrence in the Former Yugoslavia" (November 2013), European Council on Foreign Relations.

2

Legal Expertise

Implications of Legal Terminology in Diplomatic Processes

FOCUS: RWANDA

Executive summary: This case study examines the debate over the use of the term "genocide" during the crisis in Rwanda in April of 1994. It attempts to clarify how the difficulty in determining whether the situation in Rwanda constituted genocide, in the legal sense, as established by the Genocide Convention, coupled with the uncertainty about the legal implications of using the term "genocide" contributed to the flailing international response to the humanitarian crisis.

The protracted deliberations among the United Nations Security Council (UNSC) member states, extending over a period of several weeks during April and May of 1994, focused on whether to maintain, augment, reduce, or withdraw UNAMIR peacekeeping forces stationed in Rwanda under UNSC Resolutions 912 and 918. It should be noted that a range of factors contributed to the indecision, and the failure to react was often linked to political rather than legal considerations, as will be discussed in more detail below. Nonetheless, the debate over the use of the word "genocide" in a Security Council resolution, and within the United States Department of State contributed to the extended deliberations among diplomats and Security Council members amid escalating violence.

While the case study does not argue that the uncertainty over legal grounds for, and implications of, the use of the term "genocide" was the key factor that delayed action during the Rwandan crisis, it offers an opportunity to examine the importance and impact of legal terminology on diplomatic deliberations, and explores the obstacles created by confusion about specific legal terms and concepts. What were the tactical and strategic considerations behind the positions of key Security Council members in the case of UNSC Resolutions 912, 918 and 925 in employing specific legal terminology? Why did the United States, for example, caution its diplomats not to use the word "genocide"? What are practical tactics and strategies for using or avoiding these terms in diplomatic contexts?

2.1 INTRODUCTION

This case study examines the impact of legal concepts and terminology on diplomatic deliberations, as illustrated by the controversy in using the term "genocide" to describe the violence in Rwanda in 1994. At the time of the Rwandan genocide, there were misunderstandings and confusion among diplomats over the application of the Genocide Convention and the duty it places on parties to prevent genocide. The Genocide Convention legally requires that intent (*dolus specialis*) "to destroy, in whole or in part, a national, ethnical, racial or religious group" must be proven in order for an act to be considered a crime of genocide. From a legal perspective, the intent is difficult to prove, and therefore as the events unfolded, international and state actors found themselves mired in a legal debate about the word "genocide," and the term "acts of genocide," in a situation in which an estimated 8,000 people were massacred in Rwanda each day for 100 days in the spring of 1994. The hesitation was compounded by the fact that some states, including the United States, were unsure for many weeks as to whether the events satisfied the legal definition of genocide and were concerned about any implications of describing the killings as "genocide," since some believed this could give rise to a legal duty to intervene, either jointly as the UNSC or as individual states. These events in 1994 predate the adoption of the Responsibility to Protect principles adopted by the world community at the 2005 World Summit, which outlines a nation's duty to "protect its populations from genocide, war crimes, crimes against humanity and ethnic cleansing, and their incitement" as well as providing the duties of the international community when this protection is not ensured.

To be sure, hesitancy to use the term genocide was but one of a number of factors contributing to the slow, ineffectual response to the escalating violence in Rwanda. Critical factors included concern over the instability in the country, the earlier catastrophe met by UNOSOM II in Somalia, the limited strategic interest among some state actors for the situation in Rwanda, and the predominance of the Arusha Accords as a framework for negotiation. While the ambiguity regarding the application of international law should not be seen as the driving force behind the inaction of the international community in Rwanda, a study of events in Rwanda provides an interesting example of how confusion about legal obligations can to some extent affect diplomatic responses to a crisis. Thus, the principal concern at issue for the purpose of our case study is a limited one: how diplomats interpreted the legal term "genocide," its applicability to the Rwandan crisis, and resulting state obligations under international law, and to what extent it affected their actions.

2.2 BACKGROUND

On April 6, 1994, a plane carrying Rwandan President Juvenal Habyarimana and Burundian President Cyprien Ntarymira was shot down. The alleged perpetrators are disputed, but it is suspected that extremists in the military and government perpetrated the attack as part of their opposition to the Arusha Accords. These were a series of deals made in August 1993, after three years of war and negotiations, between Habyarimana's Hutu-led government and the Tutsi-led rebel Rwandan Patriotic Front (RPF). The Accords effectively would have ended Habyarimana's twenty-year one-party rule. Hutu extremists rejected these terms and began persecuting Tutsi as well as Hutu supporters of the Arusha peace process.

Within days of the plane crash, government forces had already begun the slaughter of Tutsis and moderate high-profile Hutus, including the opposition leader, who were seen as threats to the Hutus' dominance in politics. Over a period of three months, it is estimated that around 800,000 Rwandans were killed, making the rate of killing four times higher than at the height of the Nazi Holocaust. The victims were not just the Tutsis and moderate Hutus: it is estimated that 30 percent of the minority Twa population at the time (about 10,000 people) were also killed during the genocide. The heavily criticized failure of the international community to prevent and restrain this violence has become one of the most significant diplomatic events of the twentieth century.

Earlier, in October 1993, the UN had created the United Nations Assistance Mission for Rwanda (UNAMIR) as a peacekeeping force and to assist with the governmental transition in Rwanda after the Arusha Accords. The day after the plane crash, ten Belgian peacekeepers were brutally murdered by the presidential guard. As the violence escalated, UNAMIR attempted to intervene and to mediate between the RPF and the Rwandan army. However, on April 21, 1994, pressured by the United States and Belgium, the UNSC voted to significantly reduce UNAMIR's forces from 2,548 to 270 troops.

Faced with escalating violence and increasing international pressure from media and human rights groups, the UN reached a compromise on May 17, 1994 and created UNAMIR II, consisting of 5,500 troops. On June 15, France announced that it would intervene, an action which was approved by the UN on June 22. By the time troops entered the country, the massacre was mostly over. On July 4, the RPF took the capital and soon took control of the country. It was not until November of 1994 that the UN set up the International Criminal Tribunal for Rwanda (ICTR), which was given jurisdiction over genocides, crimes against humanity, and war crimes committed in Rwanda between January 1 and December 31, 1994. The ICTR has issued ninety-three indictments and handed down the first ever convictions of genocide in the history of international law.

The present case study looks at the way in which uncertainty about the meaning and implications of the legal term "genocide" can in some cases affect the diplomatic dialogue, taking the Rwandan case as an example.

2.3 THE TERM "GENOCIDE" AND THE CASE OF RWANDA IN 1994

This section provides evidence as to how some diplomats and other international actors misunderstood the Genocide Convention, and how that misunderstanding influenced their actions during the Rwandan genocide. Some diplomats appeared concerned that if they used the word "genocide" to describe a violent situation, they would have a legal obligation to act in some way.

2.3.1 Use by the United Nations

Three separate actors within the UN must be distinguished: the United Nations Security Council, the UN Secretary-General, and the member states of the UN.

The UNSC adopted three resolutions from the start of the killings in Rwanda genocide before the term "genocide" was used, and the President of the UNSC also issued statements agreed upon by its members. Resolution 912 was adopted on April 21, 1994 significantly reducing the scale of UNAMIR. It made no reference to genocide but did call on all concerned "to respect fully international humanitarian law." It referred to "widespread violence" and "numerous killings of civilians," calling for a "ceasefire."[1]

As the situation in Rwanda deteriorated, the UNSC felt pressured to respond to the crisis in stronger terms. On April 25, the Czech Republic Ambassador to the UN (Karel Kovanda) wrote to Prague and described the situation as genocide[2] and on April 28, he proposed a draft presidential statement which used the term.[3] However, the Czech delegation was aware of the discomfort the term genocide would cause some countries as indicated in an April 29 cable to the Foreign Ministry in Prague: "We anticipated difficulties with the term 'genocide'."[4] The draft was backed by Argentina, Brazil, Pakistan, New Zealand, and Spain.[5,6] The ambassador of New Zealand, Colin Keating, as the President of the Council at the time, took up the suggestion, proposing a statement using the language in informal discussions the next day.[7]

Keating believed that if the UNSC described the situation as genocide then those member states of the UNSC who had signed the Genocide Convention would be legally bound to act.[8] While the Genocide Convention does not stipulate what kind

---

[1]   Security Council Res. 912 (April 21, 1994), UN Doc. S/RES/912.

[2]   M.Dobbs (ed.), *Inside the UN Security Council April–July 1994* (National Security Archive Electronic Briefing Book No. 472, 2014).

[3]   L. Melvern, "The Security Council in the Face of Genocide" (2005) 3 *Journal of International Criminal Justice*, 4, p. 858.

[4]   Cable from CZ Mission to the UN and to the Czech Government (April 29, 1994).

[5]   Cable between the UK Mission to the UN and the UK Government (April 28, 1994); Cable between the CZ Mission to the UN and the CZ Government (April 28, 1994).

[6]   Cables between US Mission to the UN and US State Department (April 1994).

[7]   Cable from New Zealand Mission to the UN to the New Zealand Foreign Ministry (May 2, 1994).

[8]   Melvern, "The Security Council in the Face of Genocide," p. 858.

of action (diplomatic, economic, or military) is required of states parties, it may well be that he thought the term "genocide" could be used at least as a diplomatic tactic to force other countries to take effective action of some character. This tactic appeared to have worked, as some ambassadors adopted Keating's view of the Convention. The US Ambassador, in a cable sent to Washington, noted that "the events in Rwanda clearly seem to meet the definition of genocide" but believed that "if the Council acknowledges that, it may be forced to 'take such action under the Charter as they consider appropriate for the prevention and suppression of acts of genocide' as provided for in Article VIII."[9]

In 2014, Ambassador Hannay of the United Kingdom also pointed to another reason for the hesitation, stating that "hesitation about using the word 'genocide' relates to the fact that everyone's instructions in New York tended to come from Foreign Ministry lawyers telling them that they are not allowed to use words like genocide until there's a great deal of evidence."[10] This observation indicates another possible reason for the long deliberations over the use of the word "genocide." While the law is clear, the determination of whether there is enough evidence to prove the intent (*dolus specialis*) legally required to classify a killing as genocide, may prove challenging, especially if there is limited information from the ground.

Nonetheless, in the same statement, Hannay also noted, "You do not want to trigger the provisions of the Genocide Convention. I do not think it was a very sensible way to proceed but I do not think it made any difference to what was actually done."[11] Hannay's statement clearly indicates that – in retrospect – the Ambassador did not think that the concern over "triggering the provisions of the Genocide Convention," including the obligation to act to prevent genocide, altered the course of action taken by the UNSC. Kovanda, on the other hand, said that "if you identify something as genocide, you have to do something about it. If you do not do anything about it, you are violating the Genocide Convention as well." In his following sentence, he says "the US was certainly not ready to intervene in Rwanda," suggesting that he thought the duty to prevent under the Genocide Convention involved using military power.[12]

It is clear from the above discussion that, while there was certainly some uncertainty at the time over whether the term "genocide" was applicable to the Rwandan case, and what legal implications would stem from using it, the hesitation over the use of the legal term was not necessarily the key driver of the Security Council's response. In the end, the word "genocide" was not used because of Rwandan opposition that received support from China and non-permanent Security Council member Nigeria.[13] According to the Czech representative, permanent

---

9   Cables between US Mission to the UN and US State Department.
10   "June 2: Failure to Protect – Session 3: Inside the Security Council, April–July 1994," The National Security Archive, April 11, 2015, pp. 2–14.
11   Ibid., p.14.   12   Ibid., p. 27.
13   Cable from New Zealand Mission to the UN to the New Zealand Foreign Ministry.

Security Council members the UK and particularly France . . . were uncomfortable [with the draft]. Importantly, the opposition centered not on the legal consequences of using the term but on the political consequences supporting Hannay's view that the confusion over the legal terminology, while contributing to the prolonged deliberation, did not make a difference to actual responses. China, it appears, was concerned that the "cautious, non-specific formulation"[14] used might be read as being applicable to Tibet, while the "NAM had altogether a problem with allowing that only one party was responsible for the massacres; let alone that this responsibility be qualified as genocide."[15,16]

The final version of the presidential statement was adopted on April 30. Although it did not use the term "genocide," it did use some language from Article II of the Genocide Convention, by stating that, "the killing of members of an ethnic group with the intention of destroying such a group in whole or in part constitutes a crime punishable under international law." The inchoate nature of this language, and the discussions leading up to its adoption, made it clear that the UNSC was not ready to describe the situation as genocide. The UNSC Resolution 918, adopted on May 17, also did not use the term "genocide," but used identical language, further indicating UNSC's hesitancy to use the word.[17]

Furthermore, around the same time, the Foreign Minister of France, Alain Juppé, decided to use the term "genocide" in a meeting of the Human Rights Commission. Jean-Marc Rochereau de la Sablière, who worked in the French Foreign Ministry at the time, has since said that this "was not a legal decision, it was a decision that came from his heart."[18]

Finally, on June 8, the UNSC adopted Resolution 925, recognizing "reports indicating that acts of genocide have occurred in Rwanda."[19] In the meantime, on May 31, the United Nations Secretary-General (UNSG) had submitted a report to the UNSC which used the word genocide. The Nigerian Ambassador to the UN, Ibrahim Gambari, argued in 2014 that the reason for the long delay was that "the Secretary-General knew that if you use the word genocide, then there was an obligation to do something under the International Convention Against Genocide. The big boys were not prepared to do anything under the International Convention."[20]

2.3.2 *Specific Example: Response of the United States*

The declassification of many State Department documents on the Rwandan genocide has provided an illuminating example of the confusion surrounding the

---

[14]   Cable from CZ Mission to the UN to the Czech Government.   [15]   Ibid.
[16]   Cable from New Zealand Mission to the UN to the New Zealand Foreign Ministry.
[17]   Security Council Res. 918 (May 17, 1994), UN Doc. S/RES/918.
[18]   "June 2: Failure to Protect," pp. 2–82.
[19]   Security Council Res. 925 (June 8, 1994), UN Doc. S/RES/925.
[20]   "June 2: Failure to Protect," pp. 2–69.

Genocide Convention that was apparent in the debates within the UNSC, outlined above. The United States is a particularly important example given its major role in previous humanitarian interventions and the role it played in later interventions, as well as its permanent member status on the UNSC and its position in the international community.

David Scheffer, who served on the Deputies Committee of the National Security Council at the time, recalls that on April 12, 1994, the International Committee of the Red Cross (ICRC) "alerted US diplomats in Geneva . . . to the kind of horrific detail that should have compelled everyone to switch from evacuation mode to 'stop the killing' mode."[21] He stated that after receiving the report, there was a meeting at the State Department, during which there was talk of "acts of genocide" unfolding in Rwanda but that those officials in attendance were not prepared to say that "geno-cide" actually was occurring.[22] Scheffer pointed out that this "was a distinction without a meaningful difference for the public," but that seems to have been largely ignored. As will be discussed in more detail below, the choice to use the term "acts of genocide" may point, to some extent, to the uncertainty as to whether there were sufficient grounds, particularly regarding the *mens rea*, or specific intent, required for the crime of genocide, to legally classify the violence in Rwanda as "genocide," as well as to the hesitation regarding the legal obligation to take some action to prevent that using the term "genocide" would place on the United States under the Genocide Convention.

The word "genocide" appears to enter diplomatic cables on April 27, when Madeleine Albright, the US Ambassador to the UN, said that the events in Rwanda "clearly seem to meet" the definition of genocide.[23] On May 1, a discussion paper for an inter-agency discussion at the Department of Defense on the Rwanda situation noted that one of the points of discussion was the language to be used in relation to the situation.[24] On whether to describe the situation as genocide, the memorandum states "Be Careful. Legal at State was worried about this yesterday, genocide finding could commit USG to 'do something'." While the above statement does not unequivocally point to a concern about a strictly legal obligation under the Genocide Convention, it does indicate that the lawyers in the State Department were concerned not only about whether the crisis in Rwanda fulfilled the legal requirement of being called "genocide," but also about the possible obligation to act that using the word "genocide" would entail. As discussed above, even though such concern is not explicitly justified by the text of the Genocide Convention, it was shared by several diplomats and officials at the time.[25]

---

[21] D. Scheffer, *All the Missing Souls: A Personal History of the War Crimes Tribunals* (Princeton University Press, 2012), p. 51.

[22] Ibid., p. 522.   [23] Cables between US Mission to the UN and US State Department.

[24] Office of the Secretary of Defense, "Secret Discussion Paper: Rwanda" (May 1, 1994).

[25] Indeed it would not be until the International Court of Justice's decision in *Bosnia and Herzegovina v. Serbia and Montenegro* that an authoritative statement was given on when to trigger the obligation to prevent genocide. See *Application of the Convention on the Prevention and Punishment of the*

Around the same time, however, the term "genocide" appeared in internal documents of the US administration. An internal defense intelligence report from the Defense Intelligence Agency noted that "in addition to the random massacres of Tutsis by Hutu militias and individuals, there is an organized, parallel effort of genocide ... to destroy the leadership of the Tutsi community."[26]

On May 16, a member of the Office of the Legal Adviser at the State Department produced a draft legal analysis for the Secretary of State to assist in his decision on whether or not to publicly use the term "genocide."[27] It explained the requirements of genocide under the Convention and concluded that each of them had been met.

On May 21, various State Department officials submitted an action memorandum to the Secretary of State entitled "Has Genocide Occurred in Rwanda?"[28] It asked for authorization to say publicly that "acts of genocide have occurred" in Rwanda. Crucially, it contains this paragraph explaining the legal consequences of using the term "genocide":

> A USG statement that acts of genocide have occurred would not have any particular legal consequences. Under the Convention, the prosecution of persons charged with genocide is the responsibility of the competent courts in the state where the acts took place or an international penal tribunal (none has yet been established); the US has no criminal jurisdiction over acts of genocide occurring within Rwanda unless they are committed by US citizens or they fall under another criminal provisions of US law (such as those relating to acts of terrorism for which there is a basis for US jurisdiction).

At the same time the "Has Genocide Occurred in Rwanda?" memorandum further indicated that: "[i]f we do not seize the opportunity presented by fora such as the UNHRC to use the 'genocide' label to condemn events in Rwanda, our credibility will be undermined with human rights groups and the general public, who may question how much evidence we can legitimately require before coming to a policy conclusion."[29] The desire to use the formulation "acts of genocide" instead of "genocide" (a formulation also used in reference to Bosnia) appears to reflect a desire to "indicate that some, but not necessarily all, of the violence in Rwanda is 'genocide' within the meaning of the 1948 Genocide Convention." At the time of the genocide, the US government continued to portray the situation as one of civil war between the RPF and the Rwandan government. The concern about distinguishing between violence related to the genocide and violence related to the civil war persisted throughout this period, even after the State Department was willing to call the situation genocide. The "acts of genocide" and "genocide" distinction thus

Crime of Genocide (Bosnia and Herzegovina v. Serbia and Montenegro), Judgment [2007] ICJ Reports, p. 43.

[26] US Defense Intelligence Agency, "Defense Intelligence Report: The Rwandan Patriotic Front's Offensive" (May 9, 1994).

[27] US State Department, "Legal Analysis of the Situation in Rwanda" (May 16, 1994).

[28] US State Department, "Has Genocide Occurred in Rwanda?" (May 21, 1994).   [29] Ibid.

appears to be motivated by political rather than legal concerns to distinguish between the two types of violence taking place in Rwanda.

However, this finding, for whatever reason, did not make its way to the public until June 10, 1994. Even then, State Department spokesperson Christine Shelley muddied the issue by stating that "acts of genocide have occurred in Rwanda" and refusing to call it "genocide" when pushed by reporters.[30] This left the impression that the US government was still not ready to describe the situation as a genocide, despite the fact that press reports indicated otherwise. The complicated use of legal jargon made it seem as though the United States was trying to avoid legal obligations where it was not. Later that day, Secretary of State Warren Christopher, after having suffered considerable public pressure, finally officially used the term "genocide" in relation to Rwanda. These statements and internal discussions suggest that there was some confusion within the government as to how to classify the situation in Rwanda and to what extent that classification affected US obligations under international law. This confusion, in conjunction with a number of other concerns (including political pressures), could be said to have produced a lack of direction and action on the part of the United States during this time.

2.4 OTHER FACTORS CONTRIBUTING TO HESITANCY ON THE PART OF THE INTERNATIONAL COMMUNITY

A variety of factors contributed to indecision on the part of various key actors. These included a general lack of both national[31] and international[32] political interest in Rwanda, a lack of firsthand knowledge and information, a lack of media focus on the situation, the disruptive role Rwanda played as a non-permanent member of the UNSC at the time, and a general reluctance to act following previous interventions in Africa.

2.4.1 *Lack of Information*

For the international community to act in a timely fashion before genocidal violence erupts, great attention must be paid to signals, or "early warnings" in the

---

[30] Scheffer, *All the Missing Souls*, p. 65.

[31] According to Bruce Jones, "among the actors involved in Security Council deliberations, only France had interests in Rwanda ... At the same time that Rwanda was being discussed, Russia was seeking Security Council support for a mission in Georgia, and the United States was seeking support for a mission in Haiti. France let it be known that its support for those missions would be contingent on US and Russian support for the Rwandan operation." See B. D. Jones, *Peacemaking in Rwanda: The Dynamics of Failure* (Lynne Rienner Publishers, 2001), p. 109. On the so-called dynamics of failure in Rwanda among France, the USA, and Russia, see also M. Albright, *Madame Secretary: A Memoir* (Miramax Books, 2003), pp. 158–159; B. Mody, *The Geopolitics of Representation in Foreign News: Explaining Darfur* (Rowman and Littlefield, 2010), p. 11.

[32] M. N. Barnett, "The UN Security Council, Indifference, and Genocide in Rwanda" (1997) 12 *Cultural Anthropology*, 4, p. 560.

words of Kofi Annan.[33] As noted by some experts[34] lack of clear and accurate information coming out of Rwanda at the time contributed to the international community's hesitancy in describing the situation as genocide in Rwanda. There is some evidence to support that assertion. Keating, New Zealand's Ambassador to the UN at the time, said "[w]e were kept in the dark" and claimed that "[w]ith better information the Council might have proceeded quite differently."[35]

However, the planning of the Rwandan genocide was a complex process in which a multitude of state and non-state actors actively participated.[36] Today, it is no longer debatable whether Rwandan decision makers offered numerous signals from which the international community could infer genocidal intent: the world had sufficient information early on to know that an atrocity might happen. The best-known example of this is the "genocide fax," sent by the commander of UNAMIR Major-General, Roméo Dallaire, to the military adviser to the Secretary-General on January 11, 1994.[37] In it, Dallaire noted the existence of arms caches, a plot to assassinate Belgian UN peacekeepers and Rwandan members of parliament, and the existence of lists of Tutsis to be killed. He asked for authorization to interdict the arms caches, but this was refused by the UN Department for Peacekeeping Operations. While it is possible that, in some cases, the information remained at low levels and did not reach the decision makers, it is likely that the UN and certain member states knew for some time that violence was possible or even imminent. Nonetheless, no one could have predicted an atrocity on the scale that was eventually committed.

2.4.2 Lack of Media Attention

The information in the media affects the decisions of diplomats and policy makers, not only by providing them with information, but also by influencing public opinion. In the case of the Rwandan genocide, the press was slow to use the term "genocide" and to fully appreciate the scope of the atrocities taking place in Rwanda. An exception to this was *Liberation*, a French newspaper that published an article using the term "genocide" on April 11.[38] However, after this initial mention by

---

[33]   Kofi Annan underscored the importance of "early warning" in his 2004 Action Plan to Prevent Genocide. See K. Annan, "Action Plan to Prevent Genocide," UN Press Release, April 7, 2004. For an overview of signal theory applied to foreign policy, see J. D. Fearon, "Signaling Foreign Policy Interests: Tying Hands versus Sinking Costs" (1997) 41 *Journal of Conflict Resolution*, 1.

[34]   Cf. L. Melvern, "The Security Council in the Face of Genocide" (2005) 3 *Journal of International Criminal Justice*, 4, 848.

[35]   Ibid.

[36]   See K. Mills, "Rwanda: The Failure of 'Never Again'," in *International Responses to Mass Atrocities in Africa: Responsibility to Protect, Prosecute, and Palliate* (University of Pennsylvania Press, 2015); L. Melvern, *A People Betrayed: The Role of the West in Rwanda's Genocide* (Zen Books, 2009).

[37]   Cable from Romeo Dallaire to UN Department of Peacekeeping Operations, "Request for Protection for Informant" (January 11, 1994).

[38]   L. Melvern, "Missing the Story: The Media and the Rwandan Genocide" (2001) 22 *Contemporary Security Policy*, 3, 95.

Liberation, the word "genocide" did not feature in news reports for several weeks.[39] This hesitancy can be explained by the fact that most African correspondents had just covered elections in South Africa and then moved to Tanzania, where "the refugees became the story, not the genocide."[40] With the world's media focused elsewhere during the early stages of the genocide, diplomats faced little media pressure to formulate a suitable response.

2.4.3 *Rwanda as a Member of the UNSC and the Notion of a Civil War*

Rwanda was one of the non-permanent members of the UNSC in 1994 and thus during the entirety of the genocide. The Rwandan Ambassador was said to have "sat passively" throughout the discussions on the situation in Rwanda.[41] The Rwandan diplomat did not use the word "genocide," and was committed to convincing other UNSC members that the deaths in Rwanda were the result of a civil war. Declassified documents show that, on April 30, the Rwandan envoy persuaded other ambassadors to block the use of the word 'genocide' to describe events in Rwanda.[42]

On the other hand, the UNSC also received conflicting reports from the RPF. The RPF representative to the UN wrote to the UNSC president one week after the genocide began and stated that "a 'crime of genocide' had been committed in Rwanda and requested that the UNSC immediately establish a UN ICT and apprehend those responsible for the killings."[43] There is no indication that this information and plea were reflected in UNSC discussions at the time.

Consequently, the discussions of the situation in Rwanda were limited and prone to manipulation by the representative of Rwanda, who insisted that the deaths were the result of a civil war. As a result, "diplomats analyzed the situation in Rwanda through the prism of a conflict between two sides – the Hutu-dominated government of Rwanda and the insurgent Tutsi-led Rwandan Patriotic Front (RPF)," rather than as a genocide.[44]

2.4.4 *Reluctance to Intervene on the Part of the United States*

One must also place the Rwandan genocide in the context of prior peacekeeping operations. On May 6, 1994, President Clinton signed the Presidential Decision Directive (PDD) 25, limiting US involvement in international peacekeeping. Its final wording was already well known to US policy makers in early April when the Rwandan genocide began, as work had started on it in February 1993.[45] Eight

---

[39]   Ibid.   [40]   Ibid., 98.   [41]   Melvern, "The Security Council in the Face of Genocide," 855.
[42]   Dobbs, "Inside the UN Security Council."
[43]   Letter from the RPF Representative in New York to Dallaire, UNAMIR (June 3, 1994).
[44]   Scheffer, *All the Missing Souls*, p. 98.   [45]   Ibid., p. 58.

months later, in October 1993, the United States lost eighteen soldiers in the Battle of Mogadishu during an intervention in Somalia. This forced the staff working on PDD 25 to revisit the document "for several additional months of relatively minor revisions and extensive consultations on Capitol Hill."[46] PDD 25 required staff to follow various factors to consider US support for and participation in UN peace operations, and follow even more stringent requirements for direct American engagement. It stated, for example, that "the US will not support in the Security Council proposals for UN involvement in situations where such involvement is not viable or where it would interfere with US interests."[47] The PDD also included two pages of factors to be considered in determining whether an engagement could be supported.

Scheffer, who co-authored the PDD 25 and worked in the State Department at the time, later wrote that it "had the perverse effect of straitjacketing policy makers into denying justifiable interventions or preventive measures when the lives of hundreds of thousands of innocent civilians were at stake."[48] The Directive, along with the horrors of Somalia fresh in the minds of State Department officials, likely contributed to a reluctance to take part in any engagement that could lead to military involvement.

The evidence presented above suggests that the lack of political will to act in Rwanda stemmed from political considerations, which – however – were buttressed by confusion and misunderstanding surrounding the precise nature of legal obligations vis-à-vis the Genocide Convention.

2.5 THE TERM "GENOCIDE" AND LESSONS LEARNED AFTER RWANDA

The field of international criminal law has grown exponentially since the Rwandan genocide and the creation of the two ad hoc tribunals by the UN Security Council (the ICTR and the ICTY). However, it is the signing of the Rome Statute and with it the creation of the International Criminal Court in 2002 that has been most consequential. It is the first permanent international criminal court, and is tasked with ending impunity for the most serious crimes. The ICC has jurisdiction with respect to the crime of genocide, crimes against humanity, war crimes and the crime of aggression.[49] Although the ICC is separate from the UN, it is closely intertwined with the UN system. The ICC may exercise its jurisdiction in three circumstances: when a state party to the Rome Statute makes a referral to the ICC under Article 14; when the UNSC makes a referral under Chapter VII of the UN Charter; or when the Prosecutor initiates her own investigation under Article 15 of the Rome Statute.

---

[46]   Ibid.   [47]   US Government, Presidential Decision Directive No. 25/NSC-25 (May 3, 1994).

[48]   Scheffer, *All the Missing Souls*, p. 59.

[49]   Rome Statute of the International Criminal Court, Rome, July 17, 1998, in force July 1, 2002, 2187 UNTS 38544, Art. 5.

In addition to establishing the ICC, the world community has taken further steps to set non-binding standards regarding the responsibility of a nation and the international community to protect populations from genocide. In 2005, the UN General Assembly unanimously adopted the UN World Summit Outcome Document outlining the Responsibility to Protect (R2P) principles. In 2009, the Secretary-General published his Report on Implementing the Responsibility to Protect, indicating the following three pillars:

1. The State carries the primary responsibility for protecting populations from genocide, war crimes, crimes against humanity and ethnic cleansing, and their incitement.
2. The international community has a responsibility to encourage and assist states in fulfilling this responsibility.
3. The international community has a responsibility to use appropriate diplomatic, humanitarian and other means to protect populations from these crimes. If a state is manifestly failing to protect its populations, the international community must be prepared to take collective action to protect populations, in accordance with the Charter of the United Nations.[50]

One recourse the international community has in taking "collective action to protect populations, in accordance with the Charter of the United Nations" is for the Security Council to refer a situation to the International Criminal Court in order for the ICC to investigate whether genocide or other crimes against humanity have occurred or are occurring. Darfur stands as an example.

After Rwanda, the general sense was that, in future, it would be crucial to openly describe genocide as such in order to generate a more effective response. Certainly apologies to the Rwandan people by President Bill Clinton in March 1998,[51] Madeleine Albright in December 1997,[52] and UN Secretary-General Kofi Annan in May 1999,[53] and on the tenth anniversary in April 2004,[54] made it clear to the world that genocide must not happen again. And yet a decade after the genocide in Rwanda, the world was confronted with massive massacres in Sudan. Activists were aware of the importance of pressuring US officials to openly acknowledge the violence in Darfur as genocide. Mukesh Kapila, the UN's humanitarian coordinator for Sudan, gave an interview for BBC 4 on March 19, 2004, referring to the

---

50   Report of the Secretary-General, "Implementing the Responsibility to Protect" (January 12, 2009), UN Doc. A/63/677.
51   "Text of Clinton's Rwanda Speech," CBS News, March 25, 1998.
52   "Albright Apologizes for Failure of World to Stop Rwanda Genocide. She Pledged a Stronger US Commitment to Africa. One Goal: Advancing Peace and Basic Rights in Congo," Inquirer Washington Bureau, December 10, 1997.
53   "UN Chief Apologizes for Rwanda. He Admits Failure to Prevent 1994 Genocide," Deseret News, December 17, 1999.
54   "Rwanda Genocide 'Must Leave us Always with a Sense of Bitter Regret and Abiding Sorrow,' Says Secretary-General to New York Memorial Conference," UN Press Release, March 26, 2004.

violence as genocide. Speaking out after months of frustration at the international community's hesitance and inaction, he said: "This is ethnic cleansing, this is the world's greatest humanitarian crisis, and I don't know why the world isn't doing more about it. It is a human rights catastrophe on a par with the Rwandan genocide – the only difference being the numbers involved, not the means nor the aims."[55] Comparing the fighting to the Rwandan genocide in character, he said, "It is more than just a conflict. It is an organized attempt to do away with a group of people."

Kapila's interview was emblematic of growing concern over developments in Darfur. On April 7, 2004, President Bush condemned the "atrocities" in a statement.[56] Kofi Annan considered the possibility of "military action."[57] In July 2004, a congressional resolution called on the Bush administration to "seriously consider multilateral or even unilateral intervention to prevent genocide," should the UNSC fail to act, citing the Genocide Convention.[58] On September 18, 2004, the UNSC passed Resolution 1564, which threatened sanctions and "*Requests that the Secretary-General rapidly establish an international commission of inquiry in order immediately to investigate reports of violations of international humanitarian law and human rights law in Darfur by all parties, to determine also whether or not acts of genocide have occurred, and to identify the perpetrators of such violations with a view to ensuring that those responsible are held accountable.*"[59]

Interestingly, Secretary of State Colin Powell insisted that labelling the violence in Darfur as "genocide" would neither change US policy toward Sudan nor require further action from the United States which was already providing humanitarian relief and pressuring Khartoum. In this sense, Powell was hewing closely to the narrow legal requirement of Article I of the Genocide Convention requiring action to prevent but not specifying what kind of action is sufficient. Instead, he tasked the Coalition for International Justice with conducting a survey to determine whether a genocide was occurring in Darfur.[60] The Darfur Atrocities Documentation Team (ADT) subsequently surveyed over 1,136 Darfuri refugees in Chad.[61] The resulting report confirmed that the violence was widespread, directed at an ethnic group, and organized with the intent to destroy a particular population in at least a substantial

---

55 "Mass Rape Atrocity in West Sudan," BBC News, March 19, 2004.
56 G. W. Bush, "Atrocities in Sudan," US Department of State Archive, April 7, 2004.
57 S. Coates, "Military Action is Option for West as Time Ticks Away on Syria Peace Plan," *The Times*, February 28, 2017.
58 Senate of the US, "Declaring Genocide in Darfur" (108th Congress 2003–2004), ATS H.CON. RES.467, cl. 10.
59 "Security Council Declares Intention to Consider Sanctions to Obtain Sudan's Full Compliance with Security, Disarmament Obligations on Darfur," UN Press Release, September 18, 2004.
60 Sec. C. L. Powell, "The Crisis in Darfur: Testimony before the Senate Foreign Relations Committee," US Department of State Archive, December 9, 2004.
61 S. Totten and E. Markusen, "The U.S. Government Darfur Genocide Investigation" (2005) 7 *Journal of Genocide Research*, 2, pp. 279–290.

part. It also strongly indicated that the government was involved in the attacks. Based on this, in early September 2004, Powell acknowledged before the Senate Foreign Relations Committee that the violence in Darfur constituted genocide. This claim was repeated by President Bush during an address to the UNGA several weeks later, though it did not significantly affect US policy.[62]

However, many were not as quick to use the term "genocide." EU, Canadian, and British officials as well as UN Secretary-General Kofi Annan avoided the term for much of the duration of the conflict. Human Rights Watch (HRW) and Samantha Power also preferred the term "ethnic cleansing" since, they argued, Darfur did not involve the deliberate extermination of an ethnic group but rather its forced removal, and because it is difficult to prove the existence of genocide during a crisis. Pierre-Richard Prosper, the US Ambassador-at-Large for War Crimes Issues, referred to "indicators of genocide."[63] Whilst the atrocities appeared to correspond with the definition of "genocide" as set out by the Convention, it was difficult to prove that it was indeed a crime of intent.

Shortly after the Slobodan enquiry, the UNSC established its own commission tasked with determining if genocide was indeed occurring in Sudan. The UN Commission of Inquiry on Darfur concluded that the term "genocide" did *not* in fact apply, based on the lack of conclusive evidence that the leadership did indeed have the intention to destroy a substantial part of an ethnically defined population. However, the report did state that what was occurring was a crime against humanity, without determining that it was a crime of genocide, as a result of which the UNSC referred the situation to the ICC.[64]

Much has been written about why the UN Commission differed so significantly in its conclusion from the US enquiry, and this case study does not purport to establish which judgment reflects a more accurate assessment of the situation.[65] The important point here is that there was uncertainty over whether these facts met the definition of genocide. The disagreements about what to call the violence in Darfur aptly demonstrate that there has not only been significant confusion about which obligations the label of "genocide" might entail, but also uncertainty regarding the definition of the term itself.[66] These confusions and uncertainties

---

[62] S. Straus, "Darfur and the Genocide Debate" (2005) 84 *Foreign Affairs*, 1, pp. 123–133.

[63] "Statement of Pierre-Richard Prosper, Ambassador-At-Large For War Crimes – Issues Before The US House Of Representatives International Relations Committee, Subcommittee on Africa" (June 24, 2004).

[64] International Commission of Inquiry on Darfur, "Report of the International Commission of Inquiry on Darfur to the United Nations Secretary-General" (January 25, 2005).

[65] For an illuminating analysis and comparison between readings of the Genocide Convention by the UN Commission on Darfur and the ICTY in the *Kristic* case, see D. Luban, "Calling Genocide by its Rightful Name: Lemkin's Word, Darfur, and the UN Report" (2006) 7 *Chicago Journal of International Law*, 1.

[66] Gérard Prunier resorted to calling Darfur an "ambiguous genocide" and a "quasi-genocide." See *Darfur: The Ambiguous Genocide* (Cornell University Press, 2007.)

resulted in impediments to focused and effective policy discussions about how to end the violence: although not much controversy existed over the facts, public debate centered on the question of whether the crisis should be called "genocide" rather than concentrating on how to stop it. This, in part, answers the central question as to why, after everything leaders should have learned from Rwanda, it took so long for the international community to act. However, as was the case with the Rwandan crisis, there was a range of other issues, including political considerations that contributed to the delay. It is beyond the scope of this study to discuss them in depth.

One of the lessons to be learned from Darfur is that the Genocide Convention is less effective than some had hoped. Whilst it obliges signatories to "prevent" genocide, the law is unhelpfully ambiguous as to what exactly this entails. Darfur, like Rwanda, demonstrates that confusion and debate over the use of legal terminology directly affect diplomatic practice, and that the more legally certain diplomats are the more secure they can be in their decisions.

2.6 CONCLUSION

To conclude, knowledge and the adequate use of legal terminology play a significant role in diplomacy. Confusion surrounding legal terminology is generally not the primary reason behind certain diplomatic action (or lack thereof). Nonetheless, it can contribute to prolonging diplomatic deliberations. In particular, uncertainty as to under what (if any) legal obligations the UN and its member states find themselves is of key importance, as it may compound political hesitation.

The fact that there has been confusion at the highest level of diplomatic engagement during situations as dire as the genocide in Rwanda demonstrates the need for clarity. This case study also exposes how our understanding of genocide and the scope of the corresponding legal duties has been clarified over the last twenty years. There has been a transformation in our understanding of the Genocide Convention, along with its role in international law. The scope of the duty to prevent under the Genocide Convention has been clarified through several key developments, namely: the adoption of the Responsibility to Protect doctrine at the 2005 World Summit; the International Court of Justice 2007 ruling on whether Serbia incurred state responsibility for acts of alleged genocide;[67] the UNSC Resolutions mandating international commissions of inquiry; and the investigations by the International Criminal Court in referrals alleging genocide and other crimes against humanity. Two decades since the genocide in Rwanda, the case study underscores how the presence of an international criminal law framework can be a tool for diplomats rather than a hindrance.

---

[67] *Bosnia and Herzegovina v. Serbia and Montenegro.*

BIBLIOGRAPHY

Primary Sources

Application of the Convention on the Prevention and Punishment of the Crime of Genocide (*Bosnia and Herzegovina v. Serbia and Montenegro*), Judgment [2007] ICJ Reports 2007/2 ICJ 43.

Application of the Convention on the Prevention and Punishment of the Crime of Genocide (*Croatia v. Serbia*), Judgment [2015] ICJ Reports 118 ICJ 1.

Bush G. W., "Atrocities in Sudan" US Department of State Archive, April 7, 2004, available at http://2001–2009.state.gov/s/wci/us_releases/rm/31351.htm.

Convention on the Prevention and Punishment of the Crime of Genocide, Paris, December 9, 1948, in force January 12, 1951, 78 UNTS 277.

International Criminal Court (ICC), "Reporting the ICC: A Practical Guide for the Media" (June 24, 2015), available at: http://www.icc-cpi.int/iccdocs/PIDS/publications/ICC_Guide_for%20Journalists_EN.pdf.

Prosecutor V. Dusko Tadic A/K/A "Dule," Decision on the Defence Motion on Jurisdiction [1995] ICTY IT-94–1–T.

Prosper P.-R., "Statement before the US House of Representatives" International Relations Committee, Subcommittee on Africa, June 24, 2004.

Senate of the US, "Declaring Genocide in Darfur" (108th Congress 2003–2004), ATS H. CON.RES.467, cl. 10.

The Prosecutor v. Jean Kambanda, Judgment and Sentence [1998] ICTR 97–23–S.

The Prosecutor v. Tihomir Blaskić, Judgment [2000] ICTY IT-95–14–T.

Prosecutor v. Zejnil Delalic, Zdravko Mucic, Hazim Delic, Esad Landzo, Judgment [1998] ICTY IT-96–21–T.

Transcript of UNSC meeting 3368, "The situation concerning Rwanda" (April 21, 1994) UN Doc. S/PV.3368.

Transcript of UNSC meeting 3377, "The situation concerning Rwanda" (May 16, 1994) UN Doc. S/Pv.3377.

United Nations Department of Public Information, "UN Secretary-General Kofi Annan's Action Plan to Prevent Genocide," April 7, 2004, UN Doc. SG/SM/9197 AFR/893.

United Nations Security Council (UNSC) Res 912 (April 21, 1994) UN Doc. S/RES/912.

UNSC Res 918 (May 17, 1994) UN Doc. S/Res/918.

UNSC Res 925 (June 8, 1994) UN Doc. S/Res/925.

UNSC Res 940 (July 31, 1994) UN Doc. S/Res/940.

UNSC Res 1556 (July 30, 2004) UN Doc. S/Res/1556.

US Senate, "The Current Situation in Sudan and the Prospects for Peace, Hearing before the Committee on Foreign Relations" (September 9, 2004) S.HRG.108–866.

Secondary Sources

Books

Albright M., *Madam Secretary: A Memoir* (New York: Miramax Books, 2003).

Goldstone R., *For Humanity: Reflections of a War Crimes Investigator* (New Haven: Yale University Press, 2000).

Hagan J., *Justice in the Balkans: Prosecuting War Crimes in the Hague Tribunal* (Chicago: University of Chicago Press, 2003).

Hagan J. and Rymond-Richmond W., *Darfur and the Crime of Genocide* (Cambridge: Cambridge University Press, 2009).

Jones B. D., *Peacemaking in Rwanda: The Dynamics of Failure* (Boulder, Colorado: Lynne Rienner Publishers, 2001).

Krasner S. D., *Sovereignty: Organized Hypocrisy* (Princeton: Princeton University Press, 1999).

Luttwak E. N., *Strategy: The Logic of War and Peace* (Cambridge: Harvard University Press, 2001).

Mills K., "Rwanda: The Failure of 'Never Again'" in *International Responses to Mass Atrocities in Africa: Responsibility to Protect, Prosecute, and Palliate* (University of Pennsylvania Press, 2015).

Melvern L., *A People Betrayed: The Role of the West in Rwanda's Genocide* (Zen Books, 2009).

Mody B., *The Geopolitics of Representation in Foreign News: Explaining Darfur* (Lexington Books, 2010).

Peskin V., *International Justice in Rwanda and the Balkans: Virtual Trials and the Struggle for State Cooperation* (New York: Cambridge University Press, 2008).

Quigley J., *The Genocide Convention: An International Law Analysis* (Ashgate Publishing Ltd. 2006).

Schabas W., *The UN International Criminal Tribunals. The Former Yugoslavia, Rwanda and Sierra Leone* (Cambridge: Cambridge University Press, 2006).

Scheffer D., *All the Missing Souls: A Personal History of the War Crimes Tribunals* (Princeton: Princeton University Press 2012).

Sikkink K., *The Justice Cascade: How Human Rights Prosecutions Are Changing World Politics* (New York: W.W. Norton & Company, 2011).

Articles, Chapters in Edited Volumes, and Reports

Barnett M. N., "The UN Security Council, Indifference, and Genocide in Rwanda" (1997) 12 *Cultural Anthropology* 4, pp. 551–578.

Chaon A., "Who Failed in Rwanda: Journalists or the Media?" in Thompson A. (ed.), *The Media and the Rwanda Genocide* (London: Pluto Press, 2006).

Dobbs M. (ed.), "Inside the UN Security Council: April–July 1994," National Security Archive, June 2, 2014, available at: www2.gwu.edu/~nsarchiv/NSAEBB/NSAEBB472/.

Drezner D. W., "Bargaining, Enforcement, and Multilateral Sanctions: When is Cooperation Counterproductive?" (2000) 54 *International Organization*, 1, pp.73–102.

Gattini A., "Breach of the Obligation to Prevent and Reparation Thereof in the ICJ's Genocide Judgment" (2007) 18 *European Journal of International Law*, 4, pp.695–713.

Hintjens H. M., "When Identity Becomes a Knife: Reflecting on the Genocide in Rwanda" (2001) 1 *Ethnicities*, 1, pp. 25–55.

Hurd I., "Legitimacy and Authority in International Politics" (1999) 53 *International Organization*, 2, pp. 379–408.

Jehl D., "Officials Told to Avoid Calling Rwanda Killings 'Genocide'," *New York Times*, June 10, 1994.

Kaempfer W. H. and Lowenberg A. D., "Unilateral Versus Multilateral International Sanctions: A Public Choice Perspective" (1999) 43 *International Studies Quarterly*, 1, pp. 37–58.

Kapila M., as quoted in "Mass rape atrocity in west Sudan," BBC News, March 19, 2004.

Kuperman A., "How Media Missed Rwandan Genocide," in Thompson A. (ed.), *The Media and the Rwanda Genocide* (London: Pluto Press, 2006).

Kurth J., "Humanitarian Intervention after Iraq: Legal Ideals vs. Military Realities" (2007) 50 *Orbis*, 1, pp. 87–101.

Lamp N., "Conceptions of War and Paradigms of Compliance: The 'New War' Challenge to International Humanitarian Law" (2011) 16 *Journal of Conflict and Security Law*, 2, pp. 225–262.

Martin L. L., "Credibility, Costs, and Institutions: Cooperation on Economic Sanctions" (1993) 45 *World Politics*, 3, pp. 406–432.

Meernik J., "Justice and Peace? How the International Criminal Tribunal Affects Societal Peace in Bosnia" (2005) 42 *Journal of Peace Research*, 3, pp. 271–289.

Melvern L., "The Security Council in the Face of Genocide" (2005) 3 *Journal of International Criminal Justice*, 4, pp. 847–860.

Orentlicher D., "Criminalizing Hate Speech in the Crucible of Trial: *Prosecutor v. Nahimana*" (2006) 21 *American University International Law Review*, 557, pp.557–597.

Power S., "Bystanders to Genocide" (2001) *Atlantic Monthly*.

Schabas W. A., "Introductory Note to the Convention on the Prevention and Punishment of the Crime of Genocide," December 9, 1948, available at: http://legal.un.org/avl/ha/cppcg/cppcg.html.

Schimmel N., "An invisible Genocide: How the Western Media Failed to Report the 1994 Rwandan Genocide of the Tutsi and Why" (2011) 15 *The International Journal of Human Rights*, 7, pp. 1125–1135.

Sofos S. A., "Culture, Media and the Politics of Disintegration and Ethnic Division in Former Yugoslavia" in Allen T. and Seaton J. (eds.), *The Media of Conflict: War Reporting and Representations of Ethnic Violence* (London and New York: Zed Books, 1999).

Stanton G., "Could the Rwandan Genocide have Been Prevented?" (2004) 6 *Journal of Genocide Research*, 2, pp. 211–228.

Thompson A., "Coercion Through IOs: The Security Council and the Logic of Information Transmission" (2006) 60 *International Organization*, 1, pp. 1–34.

3

Compliance

Enforcing International Arrest Warrants Through Diplomacy

FOCUS: KOSOVO

Executive summary: This case study examines the complex diplomatic and judicial processes involved in executing an international arrest warrant for sitting and former high-level government officials. On May 22, 1999, the International Criminal Tribunal for the Former Yugoslavia (ICTY) brought charges against Slobodan Milošević, then President of the Federal Republic of Yugoslavia (FRY), for crimes including genocide, war crimes, and crimes against humanity, in connection to the conflict in Kosovo. In September 2000, Milošević was defeated in presidential elections; however, the new president, Vojislav Koštunica, resisted acting on the arrest warrant and delivering Milošević to the ICTY in The Hague. In October 2000, ICTY Prosecutor Carla Del Ponte lobbied American and European leaders to make a pending one billion dollar aid package and the prospect of EU accession contingent on delivering Milošević to The Hague. It would not be until April 2001 that Slobodan Milošević was arrested in Belgrade. Nearly three months after his arrest, on June 29, 2001, Milošević was transferred to The Hague to stand trial.

This case study illustrates the central role that political and diplomatic efforts can play in enforcing compliance with international judicial orders. In so doing, it raises a number of questions about the role of political interests in the execution of arrest warrants, as well as broader issues concerning the complex dynamics between diplomatic and judicial processes around international criminal accountability: What mechanisms or other recourse exist for international courts and tribunals to enforce the execution of court orders? How can diplomats and jurists cooperate without compromising the independence of the judicial process? What are the limitations and potential for jurists "bargaining" with governments in compelling adherence to court orders? What lessons can be derived for other situations?

3.1 INTRODUCTION

A persistent challenge to the efficacy of international criminal tribunals is state (non) compliance with international judicial rulings and processes of investigation. Critics argue that compliance is likely to be low where there is no political will to enforce international orders, including arrest warrants. This may be particularly true in cases where sitting or former heads of state are the subjects of international criminal indictments. Such figures may enjoy strong domestic support that bolsters nationalist claims against the authority of an international tribunal. Furthermore, countries that have undergone recent political transitions or emerged from violent conflict – for which an international criminal tribunal was authorized to intervene – may face domestic conditions too fragile or incendiary to comply with the orders of international judges.

This case study examines the efforts surrounding the arrest and transfer of one prominent international criminal indictee – Slobodan Milošević. On May 22, 1999, the ICTY indicted Milošević and four compatriots for their alleged role in mass atrocities committed against civilian Kosovar Albanians. This study centers on the issue of "compliance" to specifically highlight the complex interactions between international institutions, foreign donors, and domestic FRY officials that ultimately led to the enforcement of ICTY arrest warrants and Milošević's transfer to The Hague. While this case offers many rich lessons for observers of international criminal law, conflict resolution, and political transitions, we emphasize "compliance" to underscore the dynamic process of diplomatic pressure and political maneuvering that aided enforcement of the indictment. The indictment, and the FRY's subsequent intransigence vis-à-vis enforcement, set in motion a diplomatic push for conditionality whereby Serbia's foreign aid, international loans, and membership in the EU and NATO were linked to cooperation with the ICTY. In other words, to the extent the ICTY did not possess its own mechanism to arrest indicted perpetrators, the issue of compliance centers our attention on the interplay of diplomatic and judicial pressures that altered the incentives of FRY officials and, in effect, reshaped the domestic political will to enforce the international warrants. In cases where indicted high-ranking officials are unlikely to be arrested by sympathetic domestic forces, diplomacy thus becomes an indispensable tool to enforce international judicial orders.

3.2 VIOLENCE AGAINST KOSOVAR ALBANIANS AND THE ICTY INDICTMENT OF SLOBODAN MILOŠEVIĆ

In 1989, Kosovo lost the high degree of autonomy it had enjoyed within the former Yugoslavia. Led by then-president of Serbia, Slobodan Milošević, Serbia amended its constitution to reduce the powers of historically autonomous provinces, including Kosovo, and the legislative functions of the Kosovo Assembly in Pristina were transferred to Belgrade. Kosovar Albanians opposed these constitutional revisions and established a shadow government, even declaring an independent Republic of Kosovo. However, there was little international support for an independent state. In 1991, the European Community and Council of Ministers established the Arbitration Commission of the Peace Conference on Yugoslavia ("Badinter Committee") to advise the Conference on Yugoslavia on the legal dimensions of the dissolution of the former Yugoslavia.[1] Kosovo – and the plight of ethnic Albanians more specifically – was not considered in the Badinter Committee's opinions, nor were Kosovar Albanians invited to participate in the Dayton negotiation process.

Throughout the 1990s, in the midst of the armed conflict within the former Yugoslavia, Kosovar Albanians continuously sought to restore their autonomy. As a result, the situation began to escalate on both sides: FRY and Serbian military and police forces launched attacks against both the Kosovo Liberation Army (KLA) fighters and the Albanian civilian population; KLA insurgents, for their part, fought against the Kosovo Serb population. On January 15, 1999, a full-scale attack on the village of Reçak resulted in the deaths of approximately forty unarmed Kosovar Albanian civilians. Other attacks orchestrated by the FRY and Serb forces followed: killings of Kosovo Albanians by police in Rogovo and Rakovina at the end of January; the shelling of villages and the forced expulsion of villagers in the Vushtrri/Vučitrn municipality in February and March; and a military and police offensive in Kaçanik/Kačanik in February accompanied the destruction of civilian homes allegedly in order to clear the area of the KLA.[2]

Several weeks later, from February 6 to 23, 1999, the Contact Group on the former Yugoslavia convened peace negotiations in Rambouillet, France.[3] Both the Contact Group and Russia remained hopeful that the parties could reach a negotiated settlement, with Ibrahim Rugova as the Kosovar Albanian leader. But Rugova fell from grace and the KLA came to lead the Kosovar delegation, heeding calls by Kosovo Albanians for full independence.[4] The talks ultimately failed when the Serb and Russian delegations refused to sign the Accords (which proposed concessions of considerable autonomy for Kosovar Albanians, though not sovereignty, ensured by the presence of a NATO-led force).[5] In March 1999, the Paris

[1]   See A. Pellet, "The Opinions of the Badinter Arbitration Committee: A Second Breath for the Self-Determination of Peoples" (1992) 3 *European Journal of International Law*, 178, pp. 178–185.
[2]   OSCE/ODIHR, "Kosovo/Kosova as Seen, as Told: An Analysis of the Human Rights Findings of the OSCE, "Kosovo Verification Mission October 1998 to June 1999" (May 12, 2003).
[3]   The Rambouillet conference was co-chaired by the French and British Foreign Ministers, Hubert Vedrine and Robin Cook, and negotiations led by the US Ambassador Christopher Hill (together with Secretary Albright at the later stage), Ambassadors Wolfgang Petritsch of the EU and Boris Mayorski of the Russian Federation. NATO supported the talks. See M. Smith, *The Kosovo Conflict: US Public Diplomacy and Western Public Opinion* (Los Angeles: Figueroa Press, 2009).
[4]   B. Mason, "Rambouillet talks 'designed to fail'," BBC News, March 19, 2000.
[5]   Lord Robertson of Port Ellen, "Kosovo one year on Achievement and Challenge" (March 21, 2000).

Peace talks were suspended when Milošević refused to accept an interim political accord for Kosovo, despite intervention by US Ambassador Richard Holbrooke and public statements by US President Clinton. Subsequently, a significant number of the FRY's armed forces gathered in and around Kosovo and launched an offensive against the ethnic Albanians that spawned summary executions, forced displacements, and arson. On March 24, 1999, the North Atlantic Council (NAC) authorized airstrikes known as "Operation Allied Force."[6] In response, the FRY government broke off diplomatic relations with the United States, France, Germany, and the United Kingdom.[7] In early April 1999, information about the Serb plan ("Operation Horseshoe") to forcibly expel Kosovar Albanians was revealed.[8]

On May 27, 1999, the ICTY issued arrest warrants for Slobodan Milošević, the President of the Federal Republic of Yugoslavia; Milan Milutinović, the President of Serbia; Nikola Sainovic, Deputy Prime Minister of the FRY; Dragoljub Ojdanić, Chief of Staff of the Yugoslav Army; and Vlajko Stojiljkovic, Minister of Internal Affairs of Serbia.[9] The indictment was based on the following charges:

1. murder, a crime against humanity, punishable under Article 5(a) of the Statute, and also a violation of the laws or customs of war, punishable under Article 3 of the Statute (namely a violation of Article 3 common to the 1949 Geneva Conventions)
2. persecutions on political, racial or religious grounds, a crime against humanity pursuant to Article 5(h) of the Statute the Tribunal;
3. deportation, a crime against humanity, punishable under Article 5(d) of the Statute of the Tribunal.[10]

The indictment alleged that, between January 1999 and late May 1999, the forces of the FRY and Serbia under the control of Milošević and four others had "planned, instigated, ordered, committed or otherwise aided and abetted in a campaign of terror and violence directed at Kosovo Albanian civilians" living in all areas of Kosovo, which resulted in the forced deportation of approximately 740,000 Kosovo

---

[6]   The Independent International Commission on Kosovo later found that the military intervention by NATO after the failure of diplomacy with the Milošević regime was "illegal but legitimate" insofar as it lacked approval by the UN Security Council, but nevertheless addressed an urgent humanitarian crisis.

[7]   "Kosovo Chronology, Timeline of events 1989–1999 relating to the crisis in Kosovo," US Department of State.

[8]   Around 350,000 Kosovars overwhelmingly Albanians, but including some Serbs, were estimated to be displaced from their homes already by the end of 1998. See OSCE/ODIHR, "Kosovo/Kosova as Seen as Told."

[9]   "President Milosevic and Four other Senior Fry Officials Indicted for Murder, Persecution and Deportation in Kosovo," ICTY Press Release, May 27, 1999, JL/PIU/403-E.

[10]   Ibid.

Albanian civilians.[11] The arrest warrant was issued and transferred to all United Nations member states and to the Confederation of Switzerland.[12]

3.3 ENDING THE CONFLICT IN KOSOVO AND THE ARREST OF MILOŠEVIĆ

On June 3, 1999, the EU envoy Martti Ahtisaari and the Russian envoy Viktor Chernomyrdin presented Milošević with peace terms that would end the devastating NATO air assault against Serb forces in Kosovo. These terms were accepted by the FRY government and the Assembly of Serbia. On June 9, 1999, NATO suspended air strikes, and the following day the United Nations Security Council (UNSC) adopted Resolution 1244 (1999) mandating UN authority over legislative, executive, and judicial functions in Kosovo.[13] On June 12, 1999, Kosovo Peace Implementation Force (KFOR) and NATO-led forces commenced operating in Kosovo.

This period for the FRY was marked by increased domestic inter-party rivalry as well as hostility toward international institutions. Bolstered by nationalist sentiment that was fanned by NATO and ICTY intervention, Milošević called for early elections in September 2000. However, Milošević misjudged the extent to which such nationalist fervor would coalesce as support for his candidacy. In fact, Milošević had grown increasingly unpopular as he clamped down on domestic opposition. Milošević was defeated in the presidential election, and in December 2000 his party lost control of parliament. A new government came to power under President Vojislav Koštunica and Prime Minister Zoran Đinić.

Regime change in the FRY brought renewed pressure to comply with the ICTY arrest warrants. On January 22, 2001, the ICTY re-issued warrants for the surrender of Milošević. Likewise, the US Congress imposed a March 31, 2001 deadline for the FRY to meet several conditions, including cooperation with the ICTY, to qualify for foreign aid.[14] Koštunica strongly opposed transferring Milošević to The Hague. Indeed, Koštunica effectively pledged not to extradite Milošević as a condition for his peaceful transfer of power.[15] On the other hand, Đinić saw further integration with Europe and the West as the path toward political and economic development in Serbia. For Đinić, cooperation with the ICTY on the Milošević indictment, however instrumental, was necessary to ensure that international aid for Serbia remained unencumbered.

[11] *The Prosecutor v. Slobodan Milošević, Milan Milutinović, Nikola Sainović, Dragolub Ojdanić, and Vlajko Stojiljković*, Indictment [1999] ICTY IT-99-37.

[12] *The Prosecutor v. Slobodan Milosević, Milan Milutinović, Nikola Sainović, Dragoljub Ojdanić & Vlajko Stojiljković*, Decision on Review of Indictment and Application for Consequential Orders [1999] ICTY IT-99-37.

[13] Security Council Res. 1244 (June 10, 1999), UN Doc. S/RES/1244.

[14] International Crisis Group, "A Fair Exchange: Aid to Yugoslavia for Regional Stability" (June 15, 2001).

[15] See "Koštunica meets Milošević," BBC News, January 14, 2001.

On April 1, 2001, Special Forces of the Serbian Interior Ministry in Belgrade arrested Milošević on charges of corruption and abuse of power. The legality of his arrest as well as his transfer to the ICTY came under some question. Ðinić ordered the arrest himself, waiting until Koštunica was out of the country and unable to prevent the order. Furthermore, upon his arrest, Milošević received assurances from Belgrade that he would only stand trial for charges before domestic courts. Nevertheless, on June 28, 2001, after domestic charges faltered, Milošević was extradited to the ICTY in The Hague.[16]

3.4 LIMITED DIPLOMACY TO ENFORCE THE ICTY'S ARREST WARRANT AGAINST MILOŠEVIĆ

This section examines efforts by international organizations – the ICTY, UNSC, and NATO – to enforce the international arrest warrant against Milošević. This analysis highlights their legal authority as well as concrete actions taken to enforce the warrant. In so doing, it foregrounds the disjuncture between intent and outcomes, that is, the challenges for enforcement where such bodies are unwilling or unable to align both domestic and international stakeholders' interests in compliance vis-à-vis international law.

3.4.1 ICTY

Prosecutor Louise Arbour submitted the indictment of Milošević on May 22, 1999. Two days later, Judge David Hunt confirmed the indictment, and on May 27 the ICTY issued a warrant for his arrest. Despite limited competence and means to enforce the warrant, Arbour's successor Carla Del Ponte and the ICTY sought assistance from UN member states, pressing for compliance particularly after Milošević's defeat in the 2000 Presidential elections. This section analyzes the ICTY's legal basis for issuing the arrest warrant. It then explores the interplay between the legal regime governing enforcement and the Tribunal's limited power to do so.

The UNSC established the ICTY by Resolution 827 (1993) passed under Chapter VII of the UN Charter for the "sole purpose of prosecuting persons responsible for serious violations of international humanitarian law committed in the territory of the

---

[16]   For an account of the complicated politics surrounding the arrest and extradition of Milošević, see C. Gall, "Serbian Tells of Spiriting Milošević Away," *The New York Times*, July 1, 2001. Ðinić was assassinated in 2003 by Serbian paramilitary unit "The Red Berets." Some conspirators explicitly attributed their motivation to Ðinić's role in supporting the ICTY investigation. See J. Subotic, "The Paradox of International Justice Compliance" (2009) 3 *The International Journal of Transitional Justice*, 9. It is also important to note that Milošević died on March 11, 2006, while on trial at The Hague. Thus, he was never formally convicted of the crimes for which he was indicted.

former Yugoslavia . . ."[17] No specific reference was made to the enforcement of such orders for arrest. However, in accordance with Article 25 of the UN Charter and the UNSC resolution, all member states are bound to cooperate with the Tribunal. The resolution also approved the ICTY Statute, which directly provides for the Tribunal to issue and to facilitate the warrants for the arrest of ICTY indictees. In particular, Article 19(2) of the Statute directly provides for the judge's authority to issue a warrant for arrest, at the request of the Prosecutor, following the confirmation of an indictment. Article 20(2) of the Statute further foresees a transfer "pursuant to an order or an arrest warrant" of the indicted person to the ICTY. Moreover, pursuant to Article 29(2) of the Statute, states are obliged to comply with the Tribunal's request for assistance or with an order issued by a Trial Chamber, including, but not limited to, orders for the arrest, detention, or the transfer of the accused to the Tribunal.

The UNSC resolution had not conferred enforcement powers upon the Tribunal, and its limited competence was affirmed by the Appeals Chamber in *Prosecutor v. Blaškić*.[18] Yet, even though the Tribunal had no means to capture an indicted person, it was vested with other legal avenues of enforcement. By virtue of Article 15 of the Statute, the Tribunal was envisaged to adopt its Rules of Procedure and Evidence (RPE) in order to conduct any "appropriate matters" at the pre-trial stage of the proceedings. When the warrant for Milošević's arrest was issued, the ICTY had the arrest procedure already in place, namely set forth in Rules 54 to 59 *bis* of the RPE. The Rules explicitly provided for the cooperation of states in executing the orders of arrest and foresaw the situation of the state's non-compliance with such enforcement. The Rules further afforded the possibility of submitting a formal notification of non compliance to the UNSC, a measure that had been exercised by the President of the Tribunal on several previous occasions.

Moreover, Rule 59 *bis* clearly authorized the Tribunal, through its Registrar and on the order of a Judge, "to transmit to an appropriate authority or international body or the Prosecutor a copy of a warrant for the arrest of an accused . . . for the prompt transfer of the accused to the Tribunal in the event that the accused be taken into

---

[17] Some interpretative guidance however, can be found in the Report of the Secretary-General pursuant to paragraph 2 of Security Council Resolution 808 on the creation of the ICTY, which stated that "an order by a TC for the surrender or transfer of persons to the custody of the ICTY shall be considered to be the application of an enforcement measure under Chapter VII of the UN Charter." See Security Council Res. 808 (May 3, 1993), UN Doc. S/25704, para. 126.

[18] In *Prosecutor v. Blaškić*, the Appeals Chamber stated as follows: "The International Tribunal does not possess any power to take enforcement measures against States. Had the drafters of the Statute intended to vest the International Tribunal with such a power, they would have expressly provided for it. In the case of an international judicial body, this is not a power that can be regarded as inherent in its functions. Under current international law States can only be the subject of countermeasures taken by other States or of sanctions visited upon them by the organized international community, i.e., the United Nations or other intergovernmental organizations." See *Prosecutor v. Tihomir Blaškić*, Judgment on the Request of the Republic of Croatia for Review of the Decision of Trial Chamber II of July 18, 1997 [1997] ICTY IT-95–14, para. 25.

custody by that authority or international body ...."[19] This Rule in particular provided inherent powers to the ICTY to demand other international bodies, such as those in the field, enforce the arrest warrant. In the Milošević case, there is no evidence that the Tribunal turned directly to any international body in the field (e.g. KFOR) in order to enforce the arrest warrant, unlike in Bosnia and Herzegovina when it sought the cooperation of national authorities and international forces (e.g. SFOR) to carry out the arrests.[20]

After the indictment of Milošević, the relationship between the Tribunal and the FRY was non-existent. The ICTY Prosecutor lacked legitimate authority to breach state sovereignty in order to arrest Milošević while he was residing in the FRY. This legal obstacle could not be overcome by the ICTY due to FRY's reluctance to submit itself to ICTY jurisdiction and due to Milošević's physical location within the state borders during the material time. This approach was tried when the ICTY Prosecutor had to use other means at her disposal. She was authorized to refer non-compliance to the UNSC in accordance with Rule 59 of the RPE and to compel the international community's assistance pursuant to Rule 61 of the RPE. This approach was tried when the ICTY's Trial Chamber pushed to compel each member of the United Nations and Switzerland to: "(i) make inquiries to discover whether any of the accused have assets located in their territory, and (ii) if any such assets are found, adopt provisional measures to freeze those assets ... until the accused are taken into custody." INTERPOL was also requested to assist in serving the arrest warrants.[21]

The ICTY made public FRY's non-compliance and general failure to cooperate with the Tribunal. For example, in November 1999, ICTY President Claude Jorda informed the UNSC of the FRY's aforementioned failure. In May 2000, Jorda made a statement to the plenary meeting of the Peace Implementation Council in which he highlighted rampant impunity for indictees due to FRY's refusal to recognize the ICTY's jurisdiction. Once Milošević was ousted from office, Jorda became even more vocal. In November 2000, he addressed the UN General Assembly (UNGA) and UNSC reminding them of the Tribunal's dependence on member states' support in arresting the accused. He asked the UN bodies to "to use all [their] influence over the member states, and more especially the successor states of the former Yugoslavia, so that they arrest and bring before the Tribunal the accused in their territory."[22]

[19]   Rules of Procedure and Evidence, July 2, 1999, IT/32/Rev.16.
[20]   Several ICTY indictees were arrested by international forces, such as SFOR, i.e. Anto Furundžija in December 1997, Goran Jelisić in January 1998, Radislav Krstič in December 1998, Zoran Vuković in December 1999 etc.
[21]   *Prosecutor v. Milošević* Decision on Review of Indictment; Report of the ICTY to the UNGA [2000] I55/273-S/20001777.
[22]   "Letter from President McDonald to the President of the Security Council concerning Outstanding Issues of State Non-Compliance," ICTY Press Release, November 2, 1999; "Statement by President Jorda to the Plenary Meeting of the Peace Implementation Council," ICTY Press Release, May 24, 2000; "Speech by his Excellency, Judge Claude Jorda, President of the International Criminal

ICTY Prosecutor Carla Del Ponte adhered to a similar approach to leverage public pressure for enforcement. On December 22, 1999, she made a public statement reassuring the international community that her top priority would be the arrest of "leading figures who were still at liberty." She committed herself to visit London, Paris and Washington, as well as NATO Headquarters in Brussels, in order to discuss the practical issues involved in implementing the arrests and transfers. Del Ponte also met with the US Secretary of State Madeleine Albright to discuss the apprehension of all remaining fugitives who had been indicted by the ICTY.[23]

On March 21, 2000, Del Ponte increased her aspirational goals to arrest Milošević and to seek assistance from the FRY's neighboring countries to accomplish this task. After Milošević's defeat in 2000, Del Ponte addressed the UNSC seeking assistance in arresting Milošević.[24] In January 2001, Del Ponte visited Belgrade and other EU governments[25] seeking to secure a non-negotiable obligation on the part of the FRY to transfer Milošević to The Hague.[26] In other words, Del Ponte seemed to recognize the limited capacity of the Office of the Prosecutor to act alone, instead seeking to rally and leverage the support of UN member states as enforcers of judicial rulings. (As discussed below, she eventually sought the adoption of policy that rendered financial/economic aid conditional on the handover of Milošević.)[27]

On April 1, 2001, Jorda and Del Ponte publicly welcomed the arrest of Milošević and referred to the positive visits of the Ministers of Justice of Serbia and the FRY to the ICTY. They both requested the authorities serve Milošević with the arrest warrant re-issued on January 22, 2001, on the basis of his indictment of May 24, 1999, relying on Rules 56 and 57 of the RPE.[28] On April 6, 2001, the ICTY Registrar handed over the indictment and the arrest warrant to the aforesaid Ministers of Justice. However, the ICTY received no confirmation on execution of that arrest warrant from the FRY authorities. In response, the ICTY Registrar threatened the

Tribunal for the former Yugoslavia, to the UN General Assembly," ICTY Press Release, November 20, 2000; "Speech by his Excellency, Judge Claude Jorda, President of the International Criminal Tribunal for the former Yugoslavia, to the UN Security Council," ICTY Press Release, November 21, 2000.

[23] "Statement by Madame Carla Del Ponte, Prosecutor of the International Criminal Tribunal for the former Yugoslavia," ICTY Press Release, November 22, 1999 and March 21, 2000; "Prosecutor Carla Del Ponte meets US Secretary of State Madeleine Albright," ICTY Press Release, May 26, 2000.

[24] "President and Prosecutor of the ICTY mandate the Registrar to travel to Belgrade," ICTY Press Release, April 1, 2001.

[25] For example, Carla Del Ponte visited officials in Rome and Brussels. See "Serbs sack Milošević judges," BBC News, February 14, 2001.

[26] Some officially uncorroborated theories alleged that the United States and several NATO states, together with Russia, were exploring ways to make a deal with Slobodan Milošević in order to escape ICTY's arrest warrant. See for example L. Sell, *Slobodan Milošević and the Destruction of Yugoslavia* (Durham: Duke University Press Books, 2002).

[27] J. R. Rudolph Jr. and W. J. Lahneman (eds.), *From Mediation to Nation-Building: Third Parties and the Management of Communal Conflict* (Lanham, Maryland: Lexington Books, 2013), pp. 192–194.

[28] "President and Prosecutor of the ICTY mandate the Registrar to travel to Belgrade," ICTY Press Release, April 1, 2001.

FRY that he would ask the UNSC to adopt the procedure for non-compliance, delineated in Rule 59(B), which potentially included sanctions if the arrest warrant went unenforced.[29]

This overview of ICTY efforts to enforce the warrant underscores the limitations of judicial power in the absence of support from member states. Moreover, it belies the notion that the indictment and arrest warrant issued against Milošević were sufficient to compel compliance. As discussed in more detail below, such efforts by the president of the Tribunal and the Office of the Prosecutor reflect a broader strategy of diplomatic engagement and external pressure on the FRY that was necessary to achieve compliance with the Tribunal's order.

3.4.2 United Nations

The UN played a substantial, albeit largely passive, role vis-à-vis the indictment and the arrest warrant against Milošević. First, the UNSC adopted Resolution 827 (1993), which established the ICTY under Chapter VII of the UN Charter and to which the ICTY's Prosecutor provided regular reports regarding her progress on investigations. Second, the UN organs, namely the UNSC and the UNGA, were sites for discussing and acting upon the FRY's reported non-compliance. Indeed, the UNSC is empowered to decide on coercive measures to compel enforcement, and the UNGA has its own competence foreseen by Article 11 of the UN Charter. Third, it was the UN (alongside other international and national actors) that liaised with the FRY regime during and after the Kosovo conflict and adopted UNSC Resolution 1244 (June 1999) that created the United Nations Interim Administration Mission in Kosovo (UNMIK). Article 14 of this resolution expressly demanded cooperation with the ICTY.

The UN was poised to play a central role in compliance with the Tribunal; however, it neither provided an enforcement mandate to the ICTY nor established a legal regime that would secure access for international forces to FRY territory (i.e. UNMIK and KFOR, which were mandated to cooperate with the ICTY). The Tribunal was vested with legal tools, i.e. referring the recalcitrant state to the UNSC. But the Security Council took a cautious approach to sanctioning noncompliance, due in large part to veto threats from Russia and China. Instead, it sought to politically isolate FRY by excluding the state from greater participation before the UN. The FRY was effectively barred from participating in the activities before UN organs. For example, during the UNSC's session of June 2000, the FRY's representative was not allowed to participate in the debate concerning FRY/Kosovo.[30] This

---

[29] "Letter from the Registrar of the International Criminal Tribunal for the former Yugoslavia, Mr. Hans Holthuis, to the Federal Minister of Justice of the Federal Republic of Yugoslavia (FRY), Mr. Homcilo Grubac," ICTY Press Release, May 3, 2001.

[30] Security Council Meeting No. 4164 (June 23, 2000), UN Doc. S/PV.4164.

was done despite the fact that the FRY had not been formally expelled or suspended from the UN.

The UNSC did occasionally respond to the ICTY's referrals concerning the FRY's non-compliance. For example, it had previously passed Resolution 1207 (1998), which demanded the "immediate and unconditional execution of those arrest warrants, including the transfer to the custody of the Tribunal."[31] However, no similar resolution was passed following the Milošević indictment. In December 2000, the UNSC adopted Resolution 1329, which *inter alia* urged all states to cooperate fully with the ICTY and its organs in accordance with their obligations under Resolution 827 (1993). Yet, it did not allow for any punitive measures in the event of non-compliance.

By contrast, the UN General Assembly was more aggressive in responding to FRY's failure to adhere to the ICTY's directives. In December 1999, at its 83rd plenary meeting, the UNGA adopted two resolutions: (1) insisting the FRY cooperate unreservedly with the ICTY; and (2) strongly denouncing the "presence of indicted war criminals in the hierarchy of the [FRY] . . . or those who are fugitives in the territory of the [FRY], and call[ing] for them to be removed from office and transferred to the custody of the [FRY] as one of the first steps towards reinstating the [FRY] in the community of law-abiding states." It also demanded that the FRY surrender those government officials of the FRY "indicted as war criminals and repudiate the leadership of anyone so indicted as a first step towards establishing a democratic government . . ."[32] In December 2000, it once again called upon the FRY to cooperate fully with the ICTY.[33]

As indicated, the UN established UNMIK by UNSC Resolution 1244 (June 1999), and placed Kosovo under its authority. The pretext for the UNSC resolution and UNMIK's establishment was discussed and prepared during the G8 summit in June 1999. The adopted conclusions were also supported by Russia – a longstanding ally of the FRY.[34] Although the conclusions raised no comments about the indictment and arrest warrant against Milošević, they did underscore the importance of

---

[31] See Security Council Res. 1207 (November 17, 1998), UN Doc. S/RES/1207, which demanded the FRY's "Immediate and unconditional execution of those arrest warrants, including the transfer to the custody of the Tribunal."

[32] General Assembly Res. 54/183 (February 29, 2000), UN Doc. A/RES/54/183; General Assembly Res. 54/184 (February 29, 2000), UN Doc. A/RES/54/184.

[33] General Assembly Res. 55/113 (March 14, 2001), UN Doc. A/RES/55/113.

[34] The official leaders of G8 summit in Cologne were the President of France J. Chirac, Chancellor of Germany G. Schröder, Prime Minister of Italy M. D'Alema, Prime Minister of Japan K. Obuchi, Prime Minister of the United Kingdom T. Blair, the President of the United States W. J. Clinton, the President of Russia B. Yeltsin, the Prime Minister of Canada J. Chrétien, and the President of the European Commission J. Santer. The Ministers of Foreign Affairs who met prior G8 meeting were L. Axworthy (Canada), H. Védrine (France), J. Fischer (Germany), L. Dini (Italy), Y. Ikeda (Japan), Y. Primakov (Russia), R. Cook (UK), M. K. Albright (USA), and H. Van Den Broek (EU). See "1999 Köln Summit: Delegations," G7 Information Centre, June 18–20, 1999.

cooperation with the ICTY.[35] Paragraph 14 of Resolution 1244 explicitly called for "full cooperation by all concerned, including the international security presence," with the ICTY.[36] Although it demanded cooperation, this specific reference remained silent with regard to enforcement of the Tribunal orders, including the warrants for arrest.[37] Moreover, the resolution restricted the presence of international security only to the territory of Kosovo and thus restricted UNMIK's law enforcement power and jurisdiction. Milošević stayed within the territory of Serbia during the material time, and Kosovo remained within the territorial boundaries of the Republic of Serbia. A strict reading of Article 29 of the ICTY Statute did not allow UNMIK's (or KFOR's) personnel to enter Belgrade and arrest Milošević, and UNSC Resolution 1244 did not include any specific mandate of operation outside the territory of Kosovo.[38] As such, UNMIK played no law enforcement role in executing the arrest warrant, as it primarily focused on the domain of security, rule of law, civilian administrative function, and development of provisional institutions for democratic self-government in the territory of Kosovo (together with the OSCE Mission in Kosovo). None of this is surprising, as it would have been entirely unrealistic for the ICTY Statute or any UN mission in Kosovo to have approved a law enforcement or military intervention onto Serbian territory for the purpose of capturing and arresting a national leader absent a UN Charter Chapter VII enforcement authority to do so.

For his part, the UN Secretary-General (SG) provided regular reports on UNMIK's operations and deployment. In these reports, the SG only made one reference to UNMIK's close cooperation with the ICTY and mentioned its support for existing indictments in 1999. However, no specific information was included concerning UNMIK's willingness to enforce any arrest warrant or its legal impediments to doing so.[39] In 2000, none of the four SG's reports presented to the UNSC made any specific reference to FRY's non-compliance with the ICTY's orders. Rather, the SG mentioned the established contacts with the authorities of the FRY through the Committee for Cooperation with UNMIK in Pristina. The

[35]   "Press Conference given by the German Foreign Minister, Mr. Joschka Fischer and G8 Foreign Ministers in Cologne," NATO Press Conferences, June 8, 1999.

[36]   Security Council Res. 1244.

[37]   During the adoption of UNSC Res. 1244, the representative of Malaysia (non-permanent member of the UNSC at the material time), directly referred to the UNSC's decision, "as contained in paragraph 14 of the resolution, which demanded full cooperation by all concerned, including the international security presence, with the Tribunal" and in substance highlighted the need for enforcing the Tribunal's orders for arrest and prosecution of indicted war criminals. He also called for the international community to be more resolute in apprehending the leading indicted war criminals as well. See Security Council Meeting No. 4011 (June 10, 1999), UN Doc. S/PV.4011.

[38]   C. K. Lamont, *International Criminal Justice and the Politics of Compliance* (Farnham: Ashgate Publishing, 2010), p. 155.

[39]   "Report of the Secretary-General on the United Nations Interim Administration Mission in Kosovo" (July 12, 1999), UN Doc. S/1999/779.

President of the Committee held regular meetings with senior representatives of UNMIK, the KFOR and other international agencies in Kosovo. Nothing in the UNSG reports suggests that the issue of the ICTY's indictments was raised during such meetings either by UNMIK or KFOR. In his two reports of 2001 (between January and June 2001), the SG marked the renewed relationship with the FRY and Serbia proper over the implementation of UNSC Resolution 1244, however limited or challenged it was. He made no specific reference to the implementation of the ICTY's orders.[40]

Although a natural site for monitoring enforcement given its role in creating the ICTY, the UN was weak in imposing real sanctions for the FRY's noncompliance. No sanctions against the FRY existed before the indictment of Milošević. Nearer the period of the Kosovo conflict, the UNSC merely adopted Resolution 1160 (1998) by which it established, *inter alia*, an embargo on arms and other materials against the FRY as a response to the excessive use of force by Serbian police force against Kosovo civilians.[41] Following the indictment, the ICTY requested UN member states and the Swiss government to freeze Milošević's assets. However, as discussed below, coercion through sanctions and aid conditionality was stronger and ultimately more effective from Europe and the United States.

3.4.3 NATO

NATO deployed its peace support operation KFOR under the authority of UNSC Resolution 1244 to support broader international efforts at peacebuilding and stabilization. Previous NATO forces deployed in the Balkan region had carried out several arrest warrants issued by the ICTY in Bosnia and Herzegovina (IFOR/SFOR). However, the NATO-led international forces engaged in Kosovo played no specific role in the enforcement of the arrest warrant against Milošević.

NATO forces were in Bosnia and Herzegovina, as set forth in the 1995 Dayton Peace Accords and UNSC Resolution 1031. However, NATO forces were not then mandated to apprehend indicted persons, and IFOR (a legal predecessor of SFOR) was "not a police force and [would] not undertake police duties."[42] However, eventually NATO forces obtained consent from local governments to exercise police powers and apprehend ICTY indictees.[43] In December 1995, the NAC adopted a

---

[40] "Report of the Secretary-General on the United Nations Interim Administration Mission in Kosovo" (March 13, 2001) UN Doc. S/2001/218; "Report of the Secretary-General on the United Nations Interim Administration Mission in Kosovo" (June 7, 2001), UN Doc. S/2001/565.

[41] Security Council Res. 1160 (March 31, 1998), UN Doc. S/RES/1160.

[42] Lamont, *International Criminal Justice*, p. 79.

[43] G. J. Knoops, *Surrendering to International Criminal Courts: Contemporary Practice and Procedure* (Transnational Publishers, 2002), p. 362.

resolution, calling on IFOR to "detain any person indicted by the ICTY who comes into contact with the IFOR in its execution of assigned tasks, in order to assure the transfer of these persons to the ICTY."[44] The ICTY and NATO also signed an agreement regarding the arrest and detention of indictees.[45]

In June 1999, the NATO Secretary-General stated that the arrest carried out by SFOR "authorize[d] SFOR to detain indicted war criminals when encountered in the course of its duties."[46] Throughout 1999 to 2001, NATO was very supportive of SFOR's arresting those individuals indicted by the ICTY.[47] However, this was not the same position held for NATO forces in Kosovo. KFOR's mandate was restricted to the territory of Kosovo. Thus, it could not enforce an arrest warrant against Milošević, who was in the territory of the FRY, and, therefore, protected by FRY's state sovereignty.[48] Some earlier statements from NATO suggested that KFOR had similar Rules of Engagement as those of SFOR, allowing the apprehension of ICTY indictees.[49] However, no additional consent or cooperation was reached between NATO allies and the FRY government in order to apprehend Milošević. Furthermore, the NAC passed no similar resolution that would authorize KFOR to execute the arrest warrants against the indictees-at-large residing in Serbia.

NATO had consistently represented that it was fully cooperating with the ICTY. However, this position was an exaggeration. NATO never adopted concrete measures to cooperate with the ICTY. For example, in June 1999 Solana announced it would be difficult to help rebuild Yugoslavia while Milošević remained in power.[50] A statement issued at the extraordinary meeting of Foreign and Defense Ministers of NAC held on June 18, 1999 suggested that NATO allies were "cooperating actively with the [ICTY] in order to bring to justice those responsible for atrocities and war crimes." However, again, though, no specific details were provided concerning such cooperation.[51] In July 1999, the

---

[44] Ibid., p. 367. The North Atlantic Council resolution was based on the General Framework Agreement for Peace in Bosnia and Herzegovina, namely Article VI, paras 4 and 5, of Annex 1-A.

[45] Cited in *Prosecutor v. Dragan Nikolić*, Decision on Defense Motion Challenging the Exercise of Jurisdiction by the Tribunal [2002] ICTY IT-94-2-PT, para. 44.

[46] "Statement by the Secretary General of NATO, Dr. Javier Solana, on SFOR's action against an indicted War Criminal," NATO Press Release, June 7, 1999.

[47] See for example "Statement by the Secretary General of NATO, Lord Robertson, on SFOR's action against indicted war criminal," NATO Press Release, December 20, 1999; "Statement by Secretary General of NATO, Lord Robertson on actions by SFOR to detain a person indicted for war crimes," NATO Press Release, December 24, 1999 and April 3, 2000.

[48] Knoops, *Surrendering to International Criminal Courts*, p. 361.

[49] "Statement to the Press by NATO Secretary General, Javier Solana following the Foreign and Defence Ministers' Meeting," NATO Press Release, June 18, 1999.

[50] "Report to Congress: Kosovo Operation Allied Force After-Action Report" (January 31, 2000).

[51] "The Situation in and Around Kosovo: Chairman's Statement issued at the Extraordinary Meeting of Foreign and Defence Ministers of the North Atlantic Council held at NATO Headquarters Brussels on 18 June 1999," NATO Press Release, June 18, 1999.

statement made by the NATO-Russia Permanent Joint Council on the Security Situation in Kosovo urged those responsible for acts of violence against the Kosovo population to be "brought to justice through the mechanisms referred to in UNSCR 1244."[52] In October 1999, following a meeting with local political leaders in Kosovo, NATO SG Lord Robertson stressed that "all parties must co-operate fully with the UN and KFOR," which included full cooperation with the ICTY in bringing war criminals to justice.[53] In December 1999, the official statement of NAC endorsed SFOR's continued strong support for the work of the ICTY, including successful arrest and transfer of those indicted for war crimes. However, in relation to KFOR's cooperation with the ICTY, no public announcement was made.[54]

Throughout the year 2000, statements by the NATO SG referred broadly to KFOR's ongoing commitment to work toward the full implementation of UNSC Resolution 1244 and "to bring war criminals to justice."[55] On several occasions, the NATO SG condemned Milošević's continuing efforts to promote and exploit ethnic division and instability in the region. However, the NATO SG failed to clearly state NATO's position towards the indictment and FRY's obligation to comply with the arrest warrant.[56] It was not until late May 2001 that NATO welcomed the arrest of Milošević and called for FRY's adherence to UNSC Resolution 1244 and full cooperation with the ICTY.[57]

Unlike previous force missions in the Balkans, NATO's KFOR was hamstrung in its capacity to arrest ICTY indictees, including Milošević. Its narrow mandate restricted operations to the Kosovo province, rendering Milošević "untouchable" in Belgrade and underscoring the necessary role of local FRY forces in his capture. Yet local forces would not cooperate on enforcement without a shift in the internal FRY incentives to cooperate with the Tribunal. The next section examines the diplomatic efforts to actively pressure the FRY government and generate political will for compliance with the ICTY order.

---

[52] "Statement by the NATO-Russia Permanent Joint Council on the Security Situation in Kosovo," NATO Press Statement, July 23, 1999.

[53] "Remarks to the Press by Secretary General, Lord Robertson," NATO Press Release, October 22, 1999.

[54] "Final Communiqué: Meeting of the North Atlantic Council in Defence Ministers Session held in Brussels," NATO Press Release, December 2, 1999; "Final Communiqué Ministerial Meeting of the North Atlantic Council held at NATO Headquarters, Brussels, on 15 December 1999," NATO Press Release, December 15, 1999; "Meeting of the North Atlantic Council in Defence Ministers Session Held in Brussels on 5 December 2000," NATO Press and Media Service, December 5, 2000.

[55] See for example NATO Press Releases, April 12, 2000, June 2, 2000, or June 8, 2000.

[56] See for example "Security Challenges in South-East Europe: Perspectives from the Region," NATO Speeches, March 26, 2001; "The State of the Alliance – A Good News Story," NATO Speeches, March 30, 2001; "Speech," NATO Speeches, May 17, 2001.

[57] "Final Communiqué: Ministerial Meeting of the North Atlantic Council Held in Budapest," NATO Press Release, May 29, 2001; or "Final Communiqué: Meeting of the North Atlantic Council in Defence Ministers Session held in Brussels," NATO Press Release, June 7, 2001.

3.5 AID CONDITIONALITY AND COMPLIANCE WITH THE ICTY

As indicated in the previous section international organizations were limited in their ability to individually spur compliance with ICTY orders. No institution alone was sufficiently imbued with the authority or resources to arrest Milošević. This section examines diplomatic efforts by the European Union and the United States to institute a policy of conditionality whereby economic aid and further integration with the West was contingent upon the FRY's cooperation with the ICTY. Such diplomacy increased external pressure on Serbian officials and was instrumental in creating political will to arrest and transfer Milošević to The Hague.

3.5.1 *European Union*

The EU pursued a two-fold diplomatic strategy to compel FRY cooperation with the ICTY. First, it adopted a longer-term negotiation strategy based on the European integration process. Second, it adopted a limited short-term policy of sanctions and aid conditionality.

While the EU prioritized regional stability in its initial engagement with the FRY,[58] it attributed full responsibility for the Kosovo crisis to Milošević and his regime and called for the ICTY to hold accountable the perpetrators of atrocities against civilians.[59] To increase pressure for accountability, EU officials retreated from engaging with the FRY concerning EU membership. The EU proposed a Stability Pact for Southeast Europe, presented in June 1999, which among other things required states to cooperate with the ICTY. The FRY was excluded from this initial stage and was only invited to participate following the October 2000 collapse of the Milošević regime. FRY participation in the integration process was linked to cooperation with the ICTY, and the EU established a commission to monitor FRY compliance. A commission working paper dated November 15, 2000 stated that lack of extradition and cooperation would "have an impact on international community efforts to assist an otherwise democratic FRY."[60] Nevertheless, the EU failed to tie FRY's compliance to any specific or concrete reward. Such abstract conditionality proved less consequential than direct financial sanctions in triggering Serbian compliance with the ICTY's arrest warrant.[61]

---

[58] It is worth noting that, from the outset, the EU's position toward Milošević was complex and somewhat ambiguous, since it directly liaised with Milošević during the Rambouillet negotiations and during the peace plan negotiations of June 1999, which were backed by the EU and led by the UN Special Envoy to Kosovo M. Ahtisaari and the Russian Envoy V. Chernomyrdin.

[59] See Security Council Meeting No. 4011 (June 10, 1999), UN Doc. S/PV.4011.

[60] International Crisis Group, "A Fair Exchange."

[61] Lamont, *International Criminal Justice*, p. 82. See also European Commission, "Communication from the Commission to the European Parliament and the Council" (October 12, 2011), COM (2011) 668 final.

Direct, explicit conditionality was more central to the EU's short-term strategy. The EU imposed several trade sanctions as the violence intensified in Kosovo, including freezing FRY assets in EU member states, as well as a ban on all new direct investment.[62] In June 1999, the EU focused on ensuring that financial transactions with persons or companies "owned and controlled by, or acting for, or on behalf of the FRY/Serbia would be blocked."[63] Later, in 2000, restrictions on financial transactions with Serbia-based companies were added.[64]

In the months preceding the autumn 2000 elections, the EU's focus shifted to regime change in Belgrade. Once Milošević was removed from power, the EU's oil embargo, imposed in May 1999, was lifted at the EU Foreign Ministers' meeting in Luxembourg. In addition, all trade and financial sanctions against the FRY were lifted save those directly concerning Milošević and other high-ranking officials.[65] Furthermore, in April 2001 the EU Commission allocated the first part of a EUR 200 million emergency aid package to help Serbia through the winter, delivery of 7,000 trucks of heating fuel, and payment of 70 percent of Serbia's electricity imports.[66] At the same time, the official request to surrender Milošević to the ICTY became more central to the EU "conditionality" agenda. Following the Milošević's arrest, the President of the European Commission, Romano Prodi, welcomed the news, stating that "Milošević must ultimately face justice for those crimes [against humanity]."[67] With the subsequent transfer of Milošević to The Hague, the EU Commission pledged a total of EUR 530 million in a financial aid package of grants and loans for the FRY at the international donors' conference, hosted jointly with the World Bank, in Brussels.[68]

[62] Lamont, *International Criminal Justice*, p. 64. See also International Crisis Group, "Sanctions against the Federal Republic of Yugoslavia" (October 10, 2000).

[63] "Council Regulation (EC) No. 1294/1999 of June 15, 1999 Concerning the Freeze of Funds and a Ban on Investment in Relation to the Federal Republic of Yugoslavia" (June 19, 1999), Official Journal L 153, pp. 0063–0082.

[64] "Council Regulation (EC) No. 723/2000 of 6 April amending Regulation of EC No. 1294/1999 Concerning a Freeze of Funds and a Ban on Investment in Relation to the Federal Republic of Yugoslavia" (April 7, 2000), Official Journal L 086, pp. 0001–004; see also International Crisis Group, "Current Sanctions Against Yugoslavia" (October 10, 2000). It is to be noted, however, that despite the EU's sanctions in place, the EU launched a program called "Energy for Democracy," through which it delivered fuel oil to several cities in Serbia, in order to lessen the impact of the economic sanctions on general population. See for example Human Rights Watch, "Federal Republic of Yugoslavia: Serbia and Montenegro" (2001).

[65] See also International Crisis Group, "Sanctions against the Federal Republic of Yugoslavia"; "Council Regulation (EC) No. 2488/2000 of November 10, 2000 maintaining a freeze of funds in relation to Mr. Milošević and those persons associated with him and repealing Regulations (EC) Nos 1294/1999 and 607/2000 and Article 2 of Regulation (EC) No. 926/98" (November 14, 2000), Official Journal L 287/19.

[66] C. Patten, "EU Strategy in the Balkans," European Commission Press Release, July 10, 2001. See also Human Rights Watch, "Serbia and Montenegro."

[67] "European Commission reacts to the arrest of Milosevic – statement by European Commission President Romano Prodi," European Commission Press Release, April 1, 2001.

[68] "European Commission pledges substantial financial support to the Federal Republic of Yugoslavia at Brussels Donors' Conference," European Commission Press Release, June 29, 2001.

3.5.2 *United States*

EU conditionality functioned in tandem with pressure on the FRY by the United States. As a driving force behind the creation of the ICTY, the United States had an interest in the effective operation of the Tribunal.[69] US involvement in the region and efforts to overcome the reluctance of states to cooperate with the ICTY intensified through its policy of aid conditionality.[70] The United States joined Germany and the United Kingdom, in particular, in diplomatic efforts to pressure the FRY to arrest Milošević. US Secretary of State Albright and German Foreign Minister Joschka Fischer "adopted a strategy that combined economic sanctions with engagement with opponents to Slobodan Milošević in Serbia itself to help bring about a change of regime in Belgrade."[71] The US strategy, operating at the Executive as well as Congressional level, focused on regime change in the FRY and on arrest and transfer of Milošević to the Tribunal. US State Department press releases and Congressional records between May 1999 and June 2001 reveal a steadfast position on FRY's obligation to comply with the ICTY in executing the Milošević arrest warrant. They further reflect a consistent view among US officials to hold Milošević criminally responsible, even before the indictment was announced.[72]

In May 1999, the US Congress discussed the issue of Milošević's alleged criminal responsibility.[73] Senator Dorgan introduced Resolution 105, citing past congressional resolutions that had condemned Serbian police actions in Kosovo and had called for the indictment of Milošević. The Resolution stated: "It is the sense of the Senate that the President should publicly declare as a matter of United States policy that the United States considers Slobodan Milošević to be a war criminal. And we urge the chief prosecutor of the International Criminal Tribunal to seek immediately an indictment of Slobodan Milošević for war crimes and to prosecute him to the fullest extent of international law."[74] Twenty-six members of the House of Representatives – Democrats and Republicans – introduced a similar concurrent resolution expressing the sense of the Congress, which *inter alia* called for a discussion with other NATO member states regarding "measures to be taken to apprehend persons indicted for war crimes and crimes against humanity" and urged "the

---

[69]   Interview with R. J. Goldstone, former Prosecutor for the ICTY in H. M. Rhea, *The United States and International Criminal Tribunals* (Intersentia, 2012), p. 131.

[70]   The United States tried to portray the ICTY as a credited legal institution and worked towards its proper functioning by using its economic leverage. In 1997 already, so to say even before the S. Milošević indictment, the United States had opposed a $30 million loan to Croatia from the World Bank in order to pressure Croatia to cooperate with the Tribunal. See Rhea, *The United States*, p. 132.

[71]   Lamont, *International Criminal Justice*.

[72]   See for example *Congressional Record: Proceedings and Debates of the 106th Congress First Session* (Washington: US Government Printing Office, 1999) Vol. 145, Pts. 8, 14; *Congressional Record: Proceedings and Debates of the 106th Congress Second Session* (Washington: US Government Printing Office, 1999), Vol. 146, Pt. 8.

[73]   *Congressional Record*, Vol. 145, Pt. 8.

[74]   US Senate Res. 105 (106th Congress, 1999–2000), ATS SRES 105.

[ICTY] to promptly review all information relating to Milosevic's possible criminal culpability, with a view toward prompt issuance of a public indictment."[75] On May 28, 1999, the day after the ICTY announced the indictments, the Treasury's Office of Foreign Assets Control, under Executive Order 13088, designated five Serbian nationals as "Specially Designated Nationals," seizing their assets and forbidding any US person to deal with those indicted persons.[76]

Furthermore, President Clinton extended US sanctions to ban oil sales and freeze Belgrade's assets in the United States. In the following month, the US State Department announced a reward of up to $5 million for information leading to the arrest or conviction in any country of persons indicted for serious violations of international humanitarian law by the ICTY. Also, in June 1999, a bill was introduced in the House of Representatives aimed at prohibiting reconstruction assistance (other than humanitarian aid) for the FRY (other than Kosovo) until Milošević and the four other indicted FRY officials "have been arrested and placed in custody of the Tribunal."[77] State Department spokesperson James Rubin underscored the Administration's commitment to enforcing the arrest warrant and affirmed the US position that harboring or granting amnesty to indicted war criminals was a violation of UN Security Council resolutions.[78]

Throughout 2000, US officials sustained public criticism of Milošević and increased pressure on the FRY to reform. In January, State Department briefings emphasized the devastating consequences of Milošević regime for the Serbian people. US officials framed Milošević as the only real obstacle to lifting sanctions and democratization in the FRY.[79] In March 2000, the United States condemned the Milošević regime's intolerance of peaceful political dissent,[80] and two months later the Senate passed a bill denouncing the undemocratic Milošević regime and expressing its sense that the United States could not "have normal relations with Belgrade as long as the Milošević regime is in power." It considered "international sanctions an essential tool to isolate the Milošević regime and promote democracy," and urged "the Administration to intensify, focus, and expand those sanctions that most effectively target the regime and its key supporters."[81] In June, US Ambassador to the UN Richard Holbrooke announced a campaign to exclude FRY from membership in the UN, and Senator Joe Biden made a strong statement on the

75 House of Representatives Con. Res. 304 (106th Congress, 1999–2000), ATS H.CON.RES.118.
76 "Serbia: Specially Designated Nationals," US Department of State Press Statement, May 28, 1999.
77 House of Representatives Bill 2187 (106th Congress, 1999–2000), HR 2187.
78 "Newsline – July 20, 1999," Radio Free Europe, July 20, 1999.
79 See for example "US Department of State Daily Press Briefing," US Department of State Archive, January 11, 2000; "Serbian Opposition Calls for Early Elections," US Department of State Press Statement, January 11, 2000.
80 "Yugoslav Harassment of Democratic Opposition," US Department of State Press Statement, March 1, 2000.
81 Senate Res. 272 (106th Congress, May 2, 2000), ATS SRES 272.

Senate floor in which he opposed any possibility of granting Milošević amnesty, criticizing a deal that had allegedly been offered by the Russian President and approved by some members of the international community.[82]

With the collapse of the Milošević regime in September 2000, the United States began to relieve sanctions in some sectors. In fact, the day after the election, the House of Representatives passed H.R. 1064, "its version of the Serbian Democratization Act ... [which] provided *inter alia* $50 million to Serbian opposition groups and [provided] $100 million for assistance to Serbia, subject to certain conditions ..."[83] In October, President Clinton announced the US intention to lift further sanctions, save those regarding the ICTY indictees. Subsequently, the United States lifted the oil embargo and flight ban to the FRY.[84]

However, sanctions remained a cornerstone of the larger US strategy to compel Milošević's arrest.[85] The annual "certification procedure" for aid to the FRY was conditioned upon FRY working with the ICTY. The US Congress required the FRY to cooperate with the ICTY by March 31, 2001, or risk losing millions in aid and possible assistance from the IMF and the World Bank.[86] The timing of Milošević's arrest by Serbian police on April 1, one day after the US certification deadline, is undoubtedly linked to this external threat and the prospect of significant costs to the FRY. When making the certification on April 2, Secretary of State Colin Powell warned that US support for an international aid conference for Serbia would depend still on Milošević's delivery to the Tribunal.[87] Likewise, on June 7, 2001, Senators Leahy and McConnell, who had introduced the bill imposing the March 31 deadline, wrote to Secretary of State Colin Powell asking for US boycott of the donors' conference unless FRY fully cooperated with the ICTY.[88] Secretary Powell echoed this concern in qualifying his certification, stressing that "the United States' support for the holding of an international donors conference for Yugoslavia would depend on the country's continued progress toward full cooperation with the tribunal."[89] To that end, President Bush reiterated that full cooperation with the Tribunal would determine if the United States would provide assistance.[90]

FRY's initial reluctance to cooperate resulted in US refusal to participate in the donor conference. The conference was eventually postponed from May to June

[82]   "Congressional Record: Against Amnesty for Milosevic" (106th Congress, 2000), Vol. 146 No. 79.
[83]   J. Kim, "Kosovo and the 106th Congress" (2001) *Congressional Research Service*.
[84]   S. D. Murphy (ed.), "Resumption of US Diplomatic Relations with the FRY" (2001) 95 *The American Journal of International Law*, 2, pp. 387–389.
[85]   See for example Human Rights Watch, "Serbia and Montenegro" and Rhea, *The United States*, p. 132.
[86]   Sell, *Slobodan Milošević and the Destruction of Yugoslavia*.
[87]   S. Woehrel, "Conditions on US Aid to Serbia" (2008) *Congressional Research Service*.
[88]   International Crisis Group, "A Fair Exchange."
[89]   "Certification of the Federal Republic of Yugoslavia," US Department of State Press Statement, April 2, 2001.
[90]   International Crisis Group, "A Fair Exchange."

2001. In response, the FRY altered its approach towards cooperation with the ICTY and made several symbolic gestures. For instance, it transferred Milomir Stakić, the former Bosnian Serb mayor of Prijedor, to the ICTY. The Federal and Serbian justice ministers, M. Momčilo Grubač and Vladan Batić, also visited The Hague.[91] The United States participated in the donors' conference in June of 2001 based on the fact that the Yugoslav and Serbian governments had started to cooperate with the ICTY.[92] The next day, Milošević (June 30, 2001) was transferred to The Hague and consequently, at the June 2001 donors conference, the United States pledged $182 million in aid to FRY.[93]

3.6 CONCLUSION

This case study illustrates how the strategic use of diplomacy can facilitate the enforcement of international arrest warrants. The indictment of Serbian leader Slobodan Milošević by the ICTY was a watershed moment for international criminal accountability. However, the indictment, for all its symbolism, merely set in motion a new, complex dynamic of diplomatic and judicial processes that ultimately led to his arrest and transfer to The Hague. The Milošević case raises questions about when and how such diplomatic efforts can lead to compliance with judicial rulings, and whether cooperation on enforcement can occur among diplomats and jurists without compromising the integrity of international justice.

A number of international stakeholders were implicated in efforts to enforce FRY's compliance with the ICTY. Such institutions, though, were individually unable and unwilling to enforce the ICTY's arrest warrant. However, this case suggests that enforcement requires a more complex, strategic use of diplomatic levers, particularly where the targets are current or former high-ranking government officials. Where there is little or no political will within a country to arrest and transfer an indictee, external pressure must be applied to shift the calculus of public officials. To be sure, FRY officials had an interest in stoking nationalist sentiment that opposed foreign intervention and compliance with the ICTY. However, FRY officials likewise had an interest in securing much-desired economic assistance and political integration with the West that would help stabilize the country over the long term. The US and EU strategy of conditionality targeted this vulnerability and effectively aligned Serbian interests in political and economic support with international interests in justice and accountability.

The Milošević case suggests that timing plays a role in defining how those diplomatic levers operate. For example, aid conditionality is more salient when

[91] Ibid.

[92] "Certification of the Federal Republic of Yugoslavia," US Department of State Press Statement, June 27, 2001.

[93] E. L Lutz and C. Reiger (eds.), *Prosecuting Heads of State* (Cambridge: Cambridge University Press, 2009). See also Human Rights Watch, "Serbia and Montenegro."

states are more dependent on foreign assistance. Similarly, EU conditionality is likely to exert more pressure to comply when national leaders are more strongly oriented toward political integration with Europe. In the FRY, Prime Minister Đinić and other Serbian politicians[94] understood the impact of FRY's exclusion from core financial assistance, since such institutions could not provide aid to non-members, and thus sought cooperation with the ICTY. In other words, diplomatic efforts can be indispensable tools for enforcing international judicial orders; however, judicial and diplomatic actors alike must understand what tools are available and how to strategically deploy them to align domestic and international interests toward compliance.

BIBLIOGRAPHY

Primary Sources

European Commission, "Communication from the Commission to the European Parliament and the Council: Commission Opinion on Serbia's Application for Membership of the European Union" (October 12, 2011), COM (2011) 668 final.

European Commission Press Release, "European Commission pledges substantial financial support to the Federal Republic of Yugoslavia at Brussels Donors' Conference," June 29, 2001.

Human Rights Watch, "Federal Republic of Yugoslavia: Serbia and Montenegro" (World Report 2001).

International Crisis Group (ICG), "A Fair Exchange: Aid to Yugoslavia for Regional Stability" (June 15, 2001).

ICG, "Sanctions against the Federal Republic of Yugoslavia (as of 10 October 2000)" (October 10, 2000).

ICTY, case of Miloševic, Slobodan (IT-02–54) "Kosovo, Croatia and Bosnia," available at: www.icty.org/case/slobodan_Milošević /4

ICTY, Seventh Annual Report (August 7, 2000) A/55/273-S/20001777.

ICTY Press Release, "Letter from President McDonald to the President of the Security Council concerning Outstanding Issues of State Non-Compliance," November 2, 1999.

ICTY Press Release, "Letter from the Registrar of the International Criminal Tribunal for the former Yugoslavia, Mr. Hans Holthuis, to the Federal Minister of Justice of the Federal Republic of Yugoslavia (FRY), Mr. Homcilo Grubac," May 3, 2001.

ICTY Press Release, "President Milošević and Four other Senior FRY Officials Indicted for Murder, Persecution and Deportation in Kosovo," May 27, 1999.

ICTY Press Release, Speech by his Excellency, Judge Claude Jorda, President of the International Criminal Tribunal for the former Yugoslavia, to the UN General Assembly, November 20, 2000.

---

[94]   The following Serbian politicians proved their positive attitude towards the policy of conditionality: Serbian Minister of Justice V. Batić, Federal Minister of Justice M. Grubač, Federal Deputy Prime Minister M. Labus, and Federal Foreign Minister Goran Svilanović. See International Crisis Group, "A Fair Exchange."

ICTY Press Release, "Speech by his Excellency, Judge Claude Jorda, President of the International Criminal Tribunal for the former Yugoslavia, to the UN Security Council," November 21, 2000.

ICTY Press Release, Statement by President Jorda to the Plenary Meeting of the Peace Implementation Council, May 24, 2000.

NATO Speeches, "Security Challenges in South-East Europe: Perspectives from the Region," March 26, 2001.

NATO Speeches, "The State of the Alliance – A Good News Story," March 30, 2001.

NATO Speeches, "Speech," May 17, 2001.

Patten C., "Speech on 'EU strategy in the Balkans'," European Commission Press Release, July 10, 2001.

Prosecutor v. Dragan Nikolić, Decision on Defense Motion Challenging the Exercise of Jurisdiction by the Tribunal [2002] ICTY IT-94-2-PT.

Prosecutor v. Tihomir Blaškic, Judgment on the Request of the Republic of Croatia for Review of the Decision of Trial Chamber II of July 18, 1997, [1997] ICTY IT-95–14.

The Prosecutor v. Slobodan Milošević, Milan Milutinović, Nikola Sainović, Dragoljub Ojdanić, and Vlajko Stojiljković, Second Amended Indictment [1999] ICTY IT-99–37-PT.

The Prosecutor v. Slobodan Milošević, Milan Milutinović, Nikola Sainović, Dragoljub Ojdanić and Vlajko Stojiljković, Decision on Review of Indictment and Application for Consequential Orders [1999] ICTY IT-99–37.

Rules of Procedure and Evidence, February 11, 1994, as amended July 24, 2009, ICTY IT/32/Rev. 43.

United Nations General Assembly (UNGA), Resolution 55/12 (November 10, 2000) UN Doc. Res A/RES/55/12.

UNGA, Resolution 54/183 (February 29, 2000), UN Doc. A/RES/54/183.

UNGA, Resolution 54/184 (February 29, 2000), UN Doc. A/RES/54/184.

UNGA, Resolution 55/113 (March 14, 2001), UN Doc. A/RES/55/113.

United Nations Security Council (UNSC), Meeting No. 4011 (June 10, 1999), UN Doc. S/PV.4011.

UNSC, Meeting No. 4164 (June 23, 2000), UN Doc. S/PV.4164.

UNSC, Statement by the President of the Security Council (March 8, 2001), UN Doc. S/PRST/2001/8.

UNSC, Resolution 1244 (June 10, 1999), UN Doc. S/RES/1244.

UNSC, Resolution 1329 (November 30, 2000), UN Doc. S/RES/1329.

UNSC, Resolution 1160 (March 31, 1998), UN Doc. S/RES/1160.

UNSC, Resolution 808 (May 3, 1993), UN Doc. S/25704.

UNSC, "Report of the Secretary-General on the United Nations Interim Administration Mission in Kosovo" (July 12, 1999), UN Doc. S/1999/779.

US House of Representatives Congress, Resolution 118 (106th Congress, 1999–2000) ATS H. Con.Res.118.

US House of Representatives Congress, Congressional Bill (106th Congress, 1999–2000), ATS H.R.2187.

US House of Representatives Congress, Congressional Bill (107th Congress, 2001–2002), ATS H.Res.200.

US Senate, Resolution 105 (106th Congress, 1999–2000), ATS S.Res.105.

US Congressional Record Senate (106th Congress, 1999–2000), 2nd Session Issue: Vol. 146, No. 79, Daily Edition June 21, 2000, available at: www.congress.gov/crec/2000/06/21/CREC-2000-06-21-pt1-PgS5549.pdf.

US Senate, Resolution 122 (107th Congress, 2001–2002), ATS S.Res.122.

US Department of State Archive, 1997–2001 Press Release, available at: http://1997–2001.state
.gov/www/briefings/statements/1999/1999_index.html.

US Department of State Archive, 2001–2009 Press Release, available at: http://2001–2009.state
.gov/r/pa/prs/dpb/index.htm.

US. Department of State Archive, "Kosovo Chronology," May 21, 1999.

US Department of State Archive, "EU Ministerial Press Conference," October 2, 2000.

Secondary Sources

Books

Arnold R., *Law Enforcement within the Framework of Peace Support Operations* (Leiden: Martinus Nijhoff Publishers, 2008).

Borger J., *The Butcher's Trail: How the Search for Balkan War Criminals Became the World's Most Successful Manhunt* (New York: Other Press, 2016).

Carter L. R., Ellis M. S. and Jalloh C. C., *The International Criminal Court in an Effective Global Justice System* (Cheltenham: Edward Elgar Publishing, 2016).

Del Ponte C., *Madame Prosecutor: Confrontations with Humanity's Worst Criminals and The Culture of Impunity: A Memoir* (New York: Other Press, 2009).

Ellis M. S., *Sovereignty and Justice: Creating Domestic War Crimes Courts within the Principle of Complementarity* (Cambridge: Cambridge Scholars Publishing, 2014).

Goldstone R., *For Humanity: Reflections of a War Crimes Investigator* (New Haven: Yale University Press, 2000).

Kerr R., *The International Criminal Tribunal for the Former Yugoslavia, an Exercise in Law, Politics, and Diplomacy* (Oxford: Oxford University Press, 2004).

Knoops G. J., *Surrendering to International Criminal Courts: Contemporary Practice and Procedure* (Ardsley: Transnational Publishers, 2002).

Lamont C. K., *International Criminal Justice and the Politics of Compliance* (Farnham: Ashgate, 2010).

Lutz E. L. and Reiger C. (eds.), *Prosecuting Heads of State* (Cambridge: Cambridge University Press, 2009).

Rhea H. M., *The United States and International Criminal Tribunals* (Mortsel: Intersentia, 2012).

Rudolph Jr. J. R. and Lahneman W. J. (eds.), *From Mediation to Nation-Building: Third Parties and the Management of Communal Conflict* (Lexington Books, 2013).

Scheffer D., *All the Missing Souls: A Personal History of the War Crimes Tribunals* (Princeton: Princeton University Press, 2012).

Sell L., *Slobodan Milošević and the Destruction of Yugoslavia* (Durham: Duke University Press Books, 2002).

Articles and Reports

"Council Regulation (EC) No. 723/2000 of April 6 amending Regulation of EC No. 1294/1999 'Concerning a Freeze of Funds and a Ban on Investment in Relation to the Federal Republic of Yugoslavia'" (April 7, 2000), Official Journal L 086, pp. 001–004.

Dobbels M., "Serbia and the ICTY: How Effective Is EU Conditionality?" (2009) *EU Diplomacy Papers* 6/2009.

Ellis M. S., "The Consequences of the Kosovo Conflict on Southeastern Europe" (2000) 34 *The International Lawyer SMU School of Law*, 4, pp. 1193–1221.

Gaeta P., "Is NATO Authorized or Obliged to Arrest Persons Indicted by the International Criminal Tribunal for the Former Yugoslavia?" (1998) 9 *European Journal of International Law*, 1, pp. 174–181.

Independent International Commission on Kosovo, *The Kosovo Report: Conflict, International Response, Lessons Learned* (Oxford: Oxford University Press, 2000).

Lamb S., "The Powers of Arrest of the International Criminal Tribunal for the Former Yugoslavia" (1999) 70 *British Yearbook of International Law*, 1, pp. 165–244.

Magliveras K. D., "The Interplay between the Transfer of Slobodan Milošević to the ICTY and Yugoslav Constitutional Law" (2002) 13 *European Journal of International Law*, 3, pp. 661–677.

Lord Robertson of Port Ellen, "Kosovo One Year on Achievement and Challenge," NATO Report (March 21, 2000).

Murphy S. D. (ed.), "Resumption of US Diplomatic Relations with the FRY" (2001) 95 *The American Journal of International Law*, 2, pp. 387–389.

Orentlicher D., *"Shrinking the Space for Denial: The Impact of the ICTY in Serbia"* (New York: Open Society Justice Initiative, 2008).

OSCE/ODIHR, "Kosovo/Kosova as Seen, as Told: An Analysis of the Human Rights Findings of the OSCE Kosovo Verification Mission October 1998 to June 1999" (May 12, 2003).

Ryngaert C., "The International Prosecutor: Arrest and Detention" (2009) *Leuven Centre for Global Governance Studies* Working Paper No. 24.

Scharf M. P., "The Tools for Enforcing International Criminal Justice in the New Millennium: Lessons from the Yugoslavia Tribunal" (2000) 49 *DePaul Law Review*, 4.

Scheffer D. J., *"Perspectives on the Enforcement of International Humanitarian Law,"* New York University School of Law (New York, February 3, 1999). Lecture available at: www.state.gov/1997-2001-NOPDFS/policy_remarks/1999/990203_scheffer_hauser.html

Smith M., "The Kosovo Conflict: US Public Diplomacy and Western Public Opinion" (2009) *CPD Perspectives on Public Policy*, Paper 3.

Strohmeyer H., "Making Multilateral Interventions Work: The UN and the Creation of Transitional Justice Systems in Kosovo and East Timor" (2011) 25 *Fletcher Forum of World Affairs*, 107.

Subotic J., "The Paradox of International Justice Compliance" (2009) 3 *The International Journal of Transitional Justice*, pp. 1–22.

Zhou H., "The Enforcement of Arrest Warrants by International Forces" (2006) 4 *Journal of International Criminal Justice*, 2, pp. 202–218.

4

Timing and Signaling

Implications of Judicial and Diplomatic Processes

FOCUS: DARFUR

Executive summary: This case study examines the complexities and signals that resulted from the timing of the March 31, 2005, UN Security Council Resolution 1593 referring the humanitarian crisis in Darfur to the Office of the Prosecutor at the International Criminal Court in The Hague. The referral occurred three months after the signing of a Comprehensive Peace Agreement that was intended to end decades of regional conflict in Sudan.

On January 9, 2005, international negotiators completed the Comprehensive Peace Agreement (CPA) between the Government of the Republic of Sudan (GoS) and the Sudan People's Liberation Army/Movement (SPLA/M). On its signature, the CPA was internationally greeted as a historic accomplishment, for it promised to bring to an end decades of regional conflict in southern Sudan – a conflict that had claimed hundreds of thousands of lives. Less than three months later, on March 31, 2005, the UN Security Council, on the recommendation of an international commission of enquiry, passed Resolution 1593, referring the situation in Darfur to the Prosecutor of the International Criminal Court. The Darfur referral – the first case referred to the ICC by the UNSC under Article 13(b) of the Rome Statute – was also the first case concerning a non-party to the Rome Statute. The subsequent investigation led to the issuance of criminal indictments against Sudan's senior leadership, including two indictments against President Omar Hassan al-Bashir, one for crimes against humanity and war crimes in July 2008, and a second for genocide, in March 2009. The timing of the two separate but interconnected processes, namely the ICC investigation seeking accountability in the "interests of justice" and diplomatic efforts to end the conflict "and guarantee lasting peace," caused myriad complications for diplomatic actions.

The case raises several critical questions: Why did the Security Council pass Resolution 1593 at such a fragile moment in the peace process? What were the diplomatic and political considerations of key state actors? What were the judicial considerations? How were the resulting signals interpreted by various parties and what were the consequences? What lessons can be derived for responses to future situations?

4.1 BACKGROUND

4.1.1 *War and Atrocities in Sudan*

In 2003, agitated by long-standing political grievances, two rebel groups, the Sudan Liberation Army (SLA) and the Justice and Equality Movement (JEM), attacked the Sudanese military and were met by a "ferocious counter-insurgency, aiming to break the back of the rebellion by destroying the insurgents' civilian support base."[1] The government attacks were spearheaded by the so-called Janjaweed militias. Because of the primarily non-Arab make-up of the rebel groups and the primarily Arab make up of the Janjaweed and the GoS, the conflict has often been viewed as being racially and ethnically motivated.[2]

Seeking to bring an end to the conflict, in 2006 the Abuja Peace Agreement was reached between the GoS and the Sudan Liberation Army.[3] However, it did not include the Justice and Equality Movement (JEM) and a splinter-group of SLA.[4] Five years later, in 2011, the Doha Peace Agreement was reached between the government and another rebel faction, the Liberation and Justice Movement.[5] While various other peace agreements and pledges to end hostilities have also been made, none conclusively resolved the conflict. Mandated by the United Nations Security Council Resolution 1769, the African Union and United Nations have deployed a hybrid peacekeeping force in Darfur since 2007.[6] Still, political violence and large-scale human suffering continue. While estimates vary, a study published in 2010 put the total number of deaths between 178,258 and 461,520. In 2007, the UN estimated that two million civilians had been displaced by the

[1] A. de Waal, "Darfur, the Court and Khartoum: The Politics of State Non-Cooperation," in N. Waddell and P. Clark (eds.), *Courting Conflict? Justice, Peace and the ICC in Africa* (London: Royal African Society, 2008), p. 29.

[2] See M. Mamdani, *Saviors and Survivors: Darfur, Politics, and the War on Terror* (Cambridge: Cambridge University Press, 2009); S. Strauss, "Darfur and the Genocide Debate" (2005) 84 *Foreign Affairs*, 1.

[3] National Legislative Bodies/National Authorities, "Darfur Peace Agreement" (May 5, 2006).

[4] On the political implications of brokering peace agreements with rebel groups in Central Africa, see A. Mehler, "Peace and Power Sharing in Africa: A Not so Obvious Relationship" (2009) 108 *African Affairs*, 432, pp. 1–21; A. Mehler, "Rebels and Parties: the Impact of Armed Insurgency on Representation in the Central African Republic" (2011) 49 *The Journal of Modern African Studies*, 1, pp. 115–139.

[5] "Draft Darfur Peace Document" (April 27, 2011).

[6] Security Council Res. 1769 (July 31, 2007), UN Doc. S/RES/1769.

conflict.[7] That number is likely much higher today, given estimates that at least 460,000 were displaced in 2013 and that over 40,000 civilians were displaced over a two-month period in February 2015.[8]

Sudan has also been the theater for another civil war, the violent political conflict between Khartoum and secessionist forces in South Sudan. After more than twenty years of hostilities, in 2005, the GoS and the SPLA agreed to the Comprehensive Peace Agreement.[9] Following a referendum in which over 98 percent of South Sudanese citizens voted for independence, South Sudan became an independent state on July 9, 2011. Despite achieving statehood, however, South Sudan continued to face internal conflict as well as bouts of political violence in the regions and provinces bordering Sudan.

4.2 GENOCIDE IN DARFUR?

As in the Rwanda case, disagreement over whether genocide was occurring in Darfur spurred a bitter debate at the international level. Disagreement was not to be found exclusively at the UN level, for even ICC officials held different views on the issue. For example, a US analyst working at the OTP "regarded the US determination that a genocide was occurring as a foregone conclusion."[10] By contrast, an African member of the ICC investigation team countered that genocidal intent was lacking, concluding that the criminal conduct which took place in the region amounted to crimes against humanity rather than genocide.[11] Surprisingly, ICC Prosecutor Moreno-Ocampo resisted calling the violence in Darfur a genocide up until June 2008, when his seventh report to the UNSC drew a direct comparison between events unfolding in that region with those which took place in the Republika Srpska in March 1995.[12]

On September 18, 2004, the United Nations Security Council, in response to the situation in Darfur, passed Resolution 1564 threatening the Sudanese government with sanctions if it did not stop the attacks by Arab Sudanese forces against black Sudanese villagers of the Darfur region. The resolution also called for a commission of inquiry to determine "whether or not acts of genocide have occurred, and to

---

[7] "The United Nations and Darfur – Fact Sheet," Peace and Security Section of the United Nations Department of Public Information (2007).

[8] "Conflict in Sudan's Darfur Displaces 41,000 in Two Months: UN," Yahoo! News, February 19, 2015; "UN: 460,000 Displaced in Darfur this Year," Al Jazeera, November 4, 2013.

[9] For the Comprehensive Peace Agreement between the government of the Republic of Sudan and the Sudan People's Liberation Movement/Sudan People's Liberation Army see "The Implementation Modalities of the Protocol on Power Sharing, Dated May 26, 2004," Reliefweb, December 31, 2004.

[10] J. Hagan and W. Rymond-Richmond, *Darfur and the Crime of Genocide* (Cambridge: Cambridge University Press, 2009), p. 33.

[11] Ibid., p. 34.

[12] ICC/OTP, "Seventh Report of the Prosecutor of the International Criminal Court to the UN Security Council Pursuant to UNSCR 1593 (2005)" (June 5, 2008), para. 93; see also Hagan and Rymond-Richmond, *Darfur and the Crime of Genocide*, p. 28.

identify the perpetrators of such violations with a view to ensuring that those responsible are held accountable."[13]

On January 25, 2005, the Commission, chaired by former ICTY president Antonio Cassese, submitted its report to the UN Secretary-General and found that international crimes had been perpetrated in Darfur. However, the Commission ultimately "concluded that the Government of the Sudan has not pursued a policy of genocide" because "the crucial element of genocidal intent appears to be missing."[14] Nevertheless, the Commission did find that "acts with genocidal intent" could have been committed but that "[w]hether this was the case in Darfur, however, is a determination that only a competent court can make."[15] The Commission strongly recommended that the situation in Darfur be referred to the ICC and provided the Court with a list of fifty-one alleged perpetrators.[16]

4.3 SIGNALING AND TIMING OF THE UNSC REFERRAL TO THE ICC

Once the wheels of international politics were finally set in motion, events followed rapidly. Just over two months after the Commission's report, the Security Council heeded the Commission of Inquiry's advice and referred the situation in Darfur to the ICC.

The UNSC – and the international community as a whole – conceived of the Darfur referral as a strong, collective signal to Sudanese authorities that the latter could take action in the de-escalation (and eventually suppression) of violence in the region. The stated end of de-escalating and suppressing violence resonates well with both the wording of the Genocide Convention (Article VIII in particular) and the official narrative that permeated the negotiations of the Rome Statute – a narrative according to which the global fight against impunity would bring about permanent and system-wide deterrent effects.[17]

However, the international community as a whole (including IGOs) clearly failed to devise and uphold a signaling strategy for Sudan-Darfur that was coherent and consistent over time. As a result, the Sudanese army and Janjaweed militias have continued to pursue their genocidal enterprise.

---

[13] Security Council Res. 1564 (September 18, 2004), UN Doc. S/RES/1564.

[14] International Commission of Inquiry on Darfur, "Report of the International Commission of Inquiry on Darfur to the United Nations Secretary-General" (January 25, 2005), p. 4.

[15] Ibid. [16] Ibid., p. 5.

[17] In his remarks on the Rome Statute's entry into force, then UN Secretary-General Kofi Annan expressed his hope that the ICC "will deter future war criminals and bring nearer the day when no ruler, no state, no junta and no army anywhere will be able to abuse human rights with impunity." See M. Simons, "Without Fanfare or Cases, International Court Sets Up," *New York Times*, July 1, 2002. On general deterrence and the role of the ICC therein, see also J. F. Alexander, "The International Criminal Court and the Prevention of Atrocities: Predicting the Court's Impact" (2009) 54 *Villanova Law Review*, 1, p. 10.

Sudan had been given mixed signals before Resolution 1593 was drafted. Both the US Congress[18] and the first George W. Bush administration with the testimony of then Secretary of State Colin Powell before the Senate Foreign Relations Committee concluded that the violence occurring in Darfur was genocide.[19] In reaching that conclusion, they relied on a wealth of intelligence, including a victimization survey of over 1,100 refugees who fled to Chad commissioned by the State Department in July 2004.[20]

The Commission of Inquiry on Darfur reached a different conclusion on genocide. It did not depend on the evidence reviewed, nor was it a function of the different interpretation adopted by legal experts in reviewing that evidence. Commission members knew the genocide's special intent was difficult to ascertain in abstract, and the case law on genocide supported their prudence. For criminal lawyers, the *mens rea* element must be proven in court and attached to one or more defendants.

The UNSC decision to refer the situation in Darfur to the ICC was certainly a historic moment, yet uncertainty on whether or not to define violence as genocide had significant consequences, many of which ultimately undermined the work of Court officials in investigating and prosecuting those responsible for it. Engineered to hold a profound and lasting impact on the mainstream understanding of state sovereignty (and sovereign immunity), the UNSC referral represents the ultimate mechanism to make the latter conditional on the external scrutiny of state behavior.[21] Furthermore, the externally imposed application of the Rome Statute onto non-parties afforded to the Security Council a powerful new tool for regime change at the domestic level. Because of the referral's implications for state sovereignty, the UNSC expected fierce opposition from states and regional organizations (e.g. the African Union) alike, so it needed a powerful narrative to overcome state concerns and have Resolution 1593 adopted. The moral high ground afforded by recognizing violence in Darfur as genocidal was a crucial element of that narrative, whereas the uncertainty on its categorization voiced by the Commission of

---

[18]   Senate of the USA, "Declaring Genocide in Darfur" (108th Congress 2003–2004) ATS H.CON. RES.467.

[19]   The US government concluded that genocide had been perpetrated in Darfur based on the evaluation of the evidence collected against the legal elements of genocide. In particular, proxies had to be used to ascertain the necessary *mens rea* element of that crime, that is, the special intent "to destroy, in whole or in part, a national, ethnical, racial or religious group, as such." The two main proxies employed were victim selection based on (perceived) ethnicity and the systematic use of racial epithets. These proxies also required a socio-historical contextualization, so their assessment had to take into account permissive conditions like the classification of social groups into an "us versus them" frame.

[20]   Hagan and Rymond-Richmond, *Darfur and the Crime of Genocide*, pp. xvii–xviii.

[21]   On the conditionality of sovereignty on state behavior, see "Secretary-General's Speech to the 54th Session of the General Assembly," UN Press Release, September 20, 1999; K. Annan, "Two Concepts of Sovereignty," *The Economist*, September 18, 1999, pp. 49–50.

Inquiry bolstered further criticism, including accusations of biased justice and undue interference in a UN member's internal affairs.

Early in 2005, the French and British ambassadors took the initiative, proposing a UNSC resolution that would refer the situation in Sudan to the ICC, even against US resistance.[22] The French mission to the UNSC under the leadership of Ambassador Jean-Marc de la Sablière stated: "... the referral to the International Criminal Court is the only solution: On the one hand because we believe in our duty to do justice to the victims, but also because acting in such a way will also allow to deter further violations. That is the reason why France has taken the initiative on this subject and why it has voted in favour of this resolution that is to be subjected to the vote of the Security Council."[23] When they canvassed their Security Council colleagues about the possibility of referring Sudan to the ICC in early 2005, the French and British ambassadors held well-founded expectations on how each country would have voted, had a specific draft resolution been tabled. Three different categories were easily identifiable: certain countries genuinely supported the referral and saw it as a way to bolster the ICC's role in the international system; others were likely to vote in favor, but had to be persuaded with side payments; the remaining countries either directly opposed the ICC or prioritized their interests in Sudan. China, Russia, and the United States belonged to this third category, and their global standing made it even more difficult to win them over. Nine out of the fifteen states sitting in the UNSC in March 2005 were parties to the Rome Statute, but that consideration was simply insufficient to craft expectations on the fate of the draft resolution once tabled.[24]

In the end, eleven states (Argentina, Benin, Denmark, France, Greece, Japan, Philippines, Romania, Russia, Tanzania, and the United Kingdom) voted in favor of Resolution 1593 referring the situation in Darfur to the ICC (March 31, 2005) whilst four abstained (Algeria, Brazil, China, and the United States). This resolution, which Sablière called "historic"[25] and a "great illustration of common Franco-British work,"[26] marked the first time a situation had been referred to the Court as well as the first time that a situation on the territory of a non-member state would fall under the jurisdiction of the ICC. In addition, the Security Council insisted, in Operative Paragraph 7 of the Resolution, that the UN would not provide funding for any "of the expenses incurred in connection with the referral,

---

[22] For the role of France, the UK and the USA in the negotiations surrounding the resolution see also C. Lesnes, "A l'ONU la Discussion sur le Jugement des Crimes Commis au Dafur Continue," *Le Monde*, March 25, 2005; J. de la Sablière, *Le Conseil de Sécurité des Nations Unies: Ambitions et Limites* (Bruxelles: Editions Larcier, 2015).

[23] See the explanation of vote on Security Council Resolution 1593, referring the situation in Darfur to the ICC "Séance Publique du Conseil de Sécurité" (March 31, 2005).

[24] Annan, "Two Concepts of Sovereignty," p. 109.   [25] "Séance Publique du Conseil de Sécurité."

[26] "Darfur/ICC Statement by the French Ambassador De la Sablière After the Vote of Resolution 1593" (March 31, 2005).

including expenses related to investigations or prosecutions in connection with that referral."[27]

4.3.1 *Key States in Favor of Resolution 1593*

United Kingdom: Despite their colonial past, the British government had neither the will nor the capacity to engage Sudan militarily. Apart from historical reasons – dating back to the nineteenth-century war against the Madhist regime and the fall of Khartoum in 1885 – in 2000 the United Kingdom was actively carrying out a policy of disengagement from its former African colonies. Against this backdrop, Prime Minister Tony Blair decided to intervene militarily in support of the legitimate government of Sierra Leone in its struggle against the Revolutionary United Front (RUF). Blair's resolve notwithstanding, British military intervention (initially labeled Operation Palliser) was minimal in terms of troops deployed and short in duration (beginning in May, the operation was virtually completed by September 2000).[28] Since humanitarian intervention in Sudan-Darfur would have had a much wider scope and thus entailed greater political and economic costs, Blair insisted on acting collectively under the UN aegis and carved out a role for the ICC as a way to demonstrate that the international community had begun addressing the Darfur crisis.[29]

France: France and the United Kingdom had jointly engineered the referral of Sudan to the ICC, and both were unwilling to act militarily against Khartoum. But France had additional reasons to justify its stance on this matter. First, Sudan did not "belong" to its sphere of influence, so France did not feel compelled to intervene in order to uphold its role of major power in that region.[30] Second, the ongoing intervention in Côte d'Ivoire was draining away economic and political resources

[27]   Security Council Res. 1593 (March 31, 2005) UN Doc. S/RES/1593, para. 7; the Rome Statute also refers to the prospect of UN payment for Security Council referrals to the ICC in Article 115(b): "Funds provided by the United Nations, subject to the approval of the General Assembly, in particular in relation to the expenses incurred due to referrals by the Security Council."

[28]   On the British military intervention in Sierra Leone, see P. Williams, "Fighting for Freetown: British Military Intervention in Sierra Leone" (2001) 22 *Contemporary Security Policy*, 3, pp. 140–168. For an assessment of British military and financial commitment to Sierra Leone in 2000, see A. M. Dorman, *Blair's Successful War: British Military Intervention in Sierra Leone* (Ashgate Publishing, 2009), pp. 66, 119.

[29]   Blair's decision to intervene in Sierra Leone is also consistent with James Kurth's argument that middle-size powers like France and the United Kingdom may only take the lead in an intervention in one of their smaller former colonies, whereas they had neither the interest nor the military capacity to lead humanitarian intervention in Sudan-Darfur. See J. Kurth, "Humanitarian Intervention after Iraq: Legal Ideals vs. Military Realities" (2007) 50 *Orbis*, 1, pp. 93, 95.

[30]   On French strategic interests in Africa, see generally P. Melly and V. Darracq, "A New Way to Engage? French Policy in Africa from Sarkozy to Hollande" (2013) *Chatham House Africa*, 2013/01.

that the French government might otherwise have allocated for Darfur. Only in early 2008 did the French-led EU peacekeeping force (EUFOR) become operative, but these troops were deployed along the Sudanese border in Chad and northeastern Central African Republic. Thus, the EUFOR mission was seemingly to contain the Darfur crisis rather than address it on Sudanese soil.[31]

Russian Federation: Perhaps the most surprising vote was cast by the Russian Federation. In explaining why Russia, which is not a party to the Rome Statute and does not support the ICC financially, had supported Resolution 1593, Ambassador Andrey Denisov declared: "Council members had reaffirmed that the struggle against impunity was one of the elements of long-term stability in Darfur. All those responsible for grave crimes must be punished, as pointed out in the report of the Commission of Inquiry."[32] Rather than a commitment to international law, however, these remarks suggested a lack of interest in undertaking more costly solutions for Sudan-Darfur. Alongside China, Russia prides itself in being a champion of state sovereignty but, unlike the former, Russia had no sizable political or economic interests in Sudan.

4.3.2 The P-5 Abstentions

United States: Dissipating hostility towards the ICC created the possibility for the United States to abstain from Resolution 1593. However, the United States also sought to tailor the referral to ensure that its citizens could not be targeted by the Court. Specifically, Operative Paragraph 6 was included to ensure that citizens of non-state parties "outside Sudan" would be excluded from investigation or prosecution by the ICC, irrespective of their conduct on the territory of Darfur "unless such exclusive jurisdiction has been expressly waived by that contributing State."[33]

China: Along with the United States, China was the other veto-wielder with major strategic interests in Sudan. What actually differed was the nature of those interests: political for the United States, economic and energy-driven for China. In fact, China is currently Sudan's first oil producer and importer, while Sudan is China's second oil exporter in Africa after Angola.[34] Concerned with preserving good

---

[31] European Union: European Security and Defence Policy, "EU Military Operation in Eastern Chad and North Eastern Central African Republic (EUFOR Tschad/RCA)" (March 2009).

[32] "Security Council Refers Situation in Darfur, Sudan, to Prosecutor of International Criminal Court," UN Press Release, March 31, 2005.

[33] Security Council Res. 1593.

[34] Even Moreno-Ocampo was well aware of China's interest in Sudanese oil. According to him, "China would abandon Bashir so long as their oil interests are protected." See D. Bosco, *Rough Justice: The International Criminal Court in a World of Power Politics* (Oxford: Oxford University Press, 2014), p. 156.

bilateral relations, many foreign policy analysts expected China to veto Resolution 1593, yet it decided to abstain. An official explanation was not forthcoming, for the Chinese ambassador did not comment on his government's choice.[35] Historically, Beijing has seldom used its veto power and, when it considered doing so, sought to act in concert with other great powers (usually Russia, less often France).[36] Vetoing a draft resolution when all other SC members will either approve or abstain is politically costly. In this specific case, Beijing likely concluded that shielding Sudan from ICC scrutiny was not worth the reputational costs of sinking collective action.[37]

4.4 ICC INDICTMENTS

In June 2005, ICC Prosecutor Luis Moreno-Ocampo announced that his office was opening an official investigation into alleged international crimes in Darfur.[38] In 2007, the Court issued warrants for two Sudanese citizens to appear before the ICC: Ahmad Haroun (Government of Sudan) on twenty counts of crimes against humanity and twenty-two counts of war crimes; and Ali Muhammad Ali Abd-Al-Rahman (known as Ali Kushayb) for twenty-two counts of crimes against humanity and twenty-eight counts of war crimes.[39] Approximately two years later, the Court issued an arrest warrant for Sudanese President Omar al-Bashir.[40] While the Prosecutor had applied to charge al-Bashir with all three Rome Statute core crimes (crimes against humanity, war crimes, and genocide), in March 2009, the ICC's Pre-Trial Chamber decided against issuing an arrest warrant for the charges of genocide. However, after the ICC Appeal's Chamber ruled that the Pre-Trial Chamber had used "an erroneous standard of proof," in July 2010, the Pre-Trial Chamber decided to issue a second arrest warrant for al-Bashir, this time for three counts of genocide.[41] In March 2012, the ICC also issued an arrest warrant for former

---

[35]   Ibid., p. 112.

[36]   On China's use of its veto power at the Security Council, see A. J. Nathan, and A. Scobell. *China's Search for Security* (Columbia University Press, 2012), pp. 29, 86, 185; D. L. Shambaugh, *China Goes Global: The Partial Power* (Oxford: Oxford University Press, 2013), pp. 83, 133, 137–142; S. L. Shirk, *China: Fragile Superpower* (Oxford: Oxford University Press, 2008), pp. 127–128.

[37]   Relatedly, Beijing eventually undermined collective action enforcement in the summer of 2008, when international media publicly blamed the Chinese government for "fueling the war" by systematically violating UN-imposed arms embargo on Darfur. See H. Andersson, "China is Fueling War in Darfur," BBC News, July 13, 2008.

[38]   See "The Prosecutor of the ICC Opens Investigation in Darfur," ICC Press Release, June 6, 2005.

[39]   *The Prosecutor v. Ahmad Muhammad Harun ("Ahmad Harun") and Ali Muhammad Ali Abd-Al-Rahman ("Ali Kushayb")* Warrant of Arrest for Ahmad Harun [2007] ICC-02/05–01/07–2.

[40]   *The Prosecutor v. Omar Hassan Ahmad Al Bashir*, Warrant of Arrest for Omar Hassan Ahmad Al Bashir [2009] ICC-02/05–01/09–1.

[41]   *The Prosecutor v. Omar Hassan Ahmad Al Bashir*, Judgment on the appeal of the Prosecutor against the "Decision on the Prosecution's Application for a Warrant of Arrest against Omar Hassan Ahmad Al Bashir" [2010] ICC-02/05–01/09–73; *The Prosecutor v. Omar Hassan Ahmad Al Bashir*, Second Warrant of Arrest for Omar Hassan Ahmad Al Bashir [2010] ICC-02/05–01/09–95.

Interior Minister and current Defence Minister Abdel Raheem Muhammad Hussein for seven counts of crimes against humanity and six counts of war crimes.[42]

In addition to government officials, the ICC also issued summonses for three rebel leaders: Bahar Idriss Abu Garda, Abdallah Banda Abakaer Nourain (Abdallah Banda), and Saleh Mohammed Jerbo Jamus (Saleh Jerbo). All appeared voluntarily before the ICC to face allegations of orchestrating lethal attacks on African Union peacekeepers. In February 2010, the Pre-Trial Chamber decided not to confirm charges against Garda.[43] The charges against Banda and Jerbo were confirmed in December 2010. However, in October 2013, proceedings against the latter were terminated following Jerbo's death. In September 2014, an arrest warrant for Banda was issued in order to ensure his presence at trial.[44] As of July 2016, he remains at-large.

4.5 FROM FORMAL COMPLIANCE TO OPEN HOSTILITY

The long-term relationship between the ICC and Khartoum is more complex than is typically assumed. Still considered to be one of the few states that voted against the Rome Statute (in part because of the UN Security Council's power to refer situations to the ICC),[45] many domestic legal and political figures initially supported Sudan joining the Court. In 2000, al-Bashir signed the Rome Statute[46] (which Sudan has not ratified).

Officially, Sudan did not refuse ICC investigators access to Darfur.[47] However, Chief Prosecutor Moreno-Ocampo was quick to declare that "[t]he security situation in Darfur means that any national or international investigations in Darfur at this time would cause risks for victims. No one can conduct a judicial investigation in Darfur."[48] As a result, the Prosecutor continued, the Court would "investigate from the outside," relying on states and NGOs and inter-governmental organizations to assist in gathering evidence.[49,50]

[42] To better understand the position held by the suspects/indictees in the Sudan-Darfur chain of command, see Hagan and Rymond-Richmond, *Darfur and the Crime of Genocide*, p. 115, and figure 5.1 in particular.

[43] *Prosecutor v. Bahar Idriss Abu Garda*, Decision on the Confirmation of Charges [2010] ICC-02/05–02/09.

[44] *The Prosecutor v. Abdallah Banda Abakaer Nourain*, Warrant of Arrest for Abdallah Banda Abakaer Nourain [2014] ICC-02/05–03/09–606.

[45] According to Antonio Cassese, Sudan cast one of the seven negative votes. See A. Cassese, *International Criminal Law* – 2nd Edition (New York: Oxford University Press, 2008), p. 330. According to David Bosco, by contrast, Sudan abstained. Bosco, *Rough Justice*, p. 50.

[46] See S. M. H. Nouwen, *Complementarity in the Line of Fire – The Catalysing Effect of the International Criminal Court in Uganda and Sudan* (Cambridge: Cambridge University Press, 2013), pp. 247–248.

[47] Ibid., p. 250; Bosco, *Rough Justice*, pp. 126–127.

[48] See W. Schabas, *An Introduction to the International Criminal Court* (Cambridge: Cambridge University Press, 2007), pp. 48–49.

[49] Ibid.

[50] B. Schiff, *Building the International Criminal Court* (Cambridge: Cambridge University Press, 2008), pp. 238–239; Schabas *An Introduction to the International Criminal Court*, pp. 49–50; Bosco, *Rough Justice*, p. 127.

Whilst vehemently opposing the surrender of any Sudanese citizens to the ICC, Sudan also welcomed at least five visits by ICC staff to Khartoum – visits conducted in order to ascertain the admissibility of any potential cases.[51] ICC staff were allowed to visit in an attempt to satisfy the ICC's complementarity regime by demonstrating that, through its creation of its Special Criminal Court, presented as a "a substitute" to the ICC, Sudan was able to investigate and prosecute alleged crimes committed in Darfur domestically.[52] However, the Office of the Prosecutor was unconvinced that the Special Criminal Court would be genuinely able or willing to prosecute government leaders responsible for atrocities and consequently pressed on with charges.[53]

All cooperation ended with the 2007 indictments of Haroun and Kushayb. According to Sarah Nouwen, communication between Sudan and the ICC was broken off and Khartoum's "Embassy in The Hague literally refused to open the door to accept the arrest warrants."[54] Any prospect of cooperation floundered further with the issuance of the first indictment for al-Bashir in 2008, precipitating a new challenge for the Court – enforcing an arrest warrant for a president intent on travelling abroad with all of the honors bestowed on a head of state.

Since the issuance of arrest warrants for al-Bashir, the Sudanese President sought to demonstrate that the warrant would not restrict his movement or diplomatic standing.[55] Some of al-Bashir's itinerary was disrupted, including plans to speak at the United Nations in New York.[56] However, al-Bashir travelled widely, his official trips including a high-profile visit to China as well as to ICC member states: Kenya, the Democratic Republic of Congo, South Africa and Chad.[57] In response, ICC Judges issued complaints of non-cooperation to the UN Security Council.[58] By March 2015, Judges ruled that Khartoum itself had "failed to cooperate with the ICC" and referred its complaint regarding Sudan's non-cooperation to the Security Council.[59]

---

[51]   Nouwen, *Complementarity in the Line of Fire*, p. 249.
[52]   See Schiff, *Building the International Criminal Court*, p. 233.   [53]   Ibid.
[54]   Nouwen, *Complementarity in the Line of Fire*, p. 250.
[55]   On the ICC's accomplishments in Sudan-Darfur, including the stigmatization of the Sudanese leadership, see A. Payam, "Are International Criminal Tribunals a Disincentive to Peace? Reconciling Judicial Romanticism with Political Realism" (2009) 31 *Human Rights Quarterly*, 3, pp. 646–652.
[56]   See L. Colum, "Sudan's Omar al-Bashir Cancels UN Trip," *Foreign Policy*, September 25, 2013.
[57]   For a detailed list of al-Bashir's post-arrest warrant travels, see Bosco *Rough Justice*, p. 158 (table 6.2 in particular).
[58]   See, e.g., *The Prosecutor v. Omar Hassan Ahmad Al Bashir*, Decision informing the United Nations Security Council and the Assembly of the States Parties to the Rome Statute about Omar Al-Bashir's presence in the territory of the Republic of Kenya [2010] ICC-02/05–01/09–107; *The Prosecutor v. Omar Hassan Ahmad Al Bashir*, Decision on the Non-Compliance of the Republic of Chad with the Cooperation Requests Issued by the Court Regarding the Arrest and Surrender of Omar Hassan Ahmad Al-Bashir [2013] ICC-02/05–01/09–151; and *The Prosecutor v. Omar Hassan Ahmad Al Bashir*, Decision on the Cooperation of the Democratic Republic of the Congo Regarding Omar Al Bashir's Arrest and Surrender to the Court [2014] ICC-02/05–01/09–195.
[59]   *The Prosecutor v. Omar Hassan Ahmad Al Bashir*, Decision on the Prosecutor's Request for a Finding of Non-Compliance Against the Republic of the Sudan [2015] ICC-02/05–01/09–227.

In the case of Darfur, the UN Security Council chose not to cooperate meaningfully with the ICC. While Resolution 1593 "urge[d] all States and concerned regional and other international organizations to cooperate fully," the Council itself has not enforced the arrest warrants issued by the Court.[60] It had also been silent with regard to the ICC's issuance of complaints of non-compliance and did nothing after it was revealed that Haroun had been transported in a helicopter paid for and arranged by the UN.[61]

Ultimately, the UN Security Council's reluctance to support the Court's mandate led to the unprecedented decision on the part of Chief Prosecutor Fatou Bensouda to "hibernate" investigations in Darfur.[62]

4.6 "PEACE VERSUS JUSTICE"

At the same time as the Security Council requested the ICC to intervene in Darfur, the Court was mired in a heated debate over its effects on "peace." The Court opened an investigation into the ongoing conflict in northern Uganda between the Lord's Resistance Army (LRA) and the Government of Uganda. Many local actors and a number of international figures responded that the ICC posed a threat to a potential peace process by removing any incentive for indicted LRA fighters to commit to negotiations.[63] Others insisted that there could be no peace without justice. In the wake of the ICC's intervention in Darfur, many pondered whether the Court would help or hinder peace in the region?[64]

The ICC arrest warrant for al-Bashir sparked "a firestorm of praise, criticism, anxiety, and relief in equal measure among peacekeepers, aid workers, diplomats and human rights activists."[65] In response to the Prosecutor's request for an arrest warrant for al-Bashir on July 14, 2008, the International Crisis Group presented a list of concerns in a report published on their website that same day:

> The Prosecutor's legal strategy also poses major risks for the fragile peace and security environment in Sudan, with a real chance of greatly increasing the suffering of very large numbers of its people. Hard-liners on all sides may be reinforced, with the governing regime and other actors reacting to today's application, and any subsequent warrant, in ways that seriously undermine the fragile North-South

---

[60] Security Council Res. 1593.

[61] M. R. Lee, "UN Says Flying ICC Indictee Haroun was in its Budget, Won't Disclose Cost," Inner City Press, February 14, 2011.

[62] *Prosecutor v. Al Bashir*, Decision on the Prosecutor's Request for a Finding of Non-Compliance against the Republic of the Sudan.

[63] See, e.g.
       T. Allen, *Trial Justice: The International Criminal Court and the Lord's Resistance Army* (London: Zed Books, 2006); A. Branch, "International Justice, Local Injustice," *Dissent Magazine*, 2004.

[64] L. Polgreen and M. Simons, "The Pursuit of Justice vs. the Pursuit of Peace," *The New York Times*, July 11, 2008.

[65] J. Geis and A. Mundt, *When to Indict? The Impact of Timing of International Criminal Indictments on Peace Processes and Humanitarian Action* (Brookings Institute: 2009), p. 1.

peace process, bring an end to any chance of political negotiations in Darfur, make impossible the effective deployment of UNAMID, put at risk the humanitarian relief operations presently keeping alive over 2 million people in Darfur, and lead to inflammation of wider regional tensions.[66]

The Sudanese government was vehemently opposed to the ICC's investigation in Darfur and explained that the Court risked undermining peace and stability in Darfur.[67] In this opinion, the Government enjoyed the support of a number of international actors.[68] The African Union (AU) declared that "the application by the ICC Prosecutor could seriously undermine the ongoing efforts aimed at facilitating the early resolution of the conflict in Darfur and the promotion of long-lasting peace."[69] China's Foreign Ministry spokesman stated that "China is opposed to any action that could interfere with the peaceful situation in Darfur and Sudan."[70]

Aggravating concerns regarding the effects of the ICC's intervention was Khartoum's expulsion of thirteen humanitarian aid groups from Darfur in the immediate aftermath of al-Bashir's indictment in March 2009. It was estimated that the international organizations expelled from Darfur employed 40 percent of all humanitarian aid workers in Darfur.[71]

While it may be convenient to use the ICC investigation as a pretext for the failure of peace negotiations and post-conflict stabilization, it is disingenuous to attribute responsibility to the ICC. The Court can be seen as fulfilling its mandate and executing its responsibilities pursuant to the Rome Statute and the UNSC referral. Any challenges to peace in the case of Darfur are not uniquely centered on the operation of the Court in this particular instance; rather, the Court's intervention brings to light problems of peace that are incumbent upon political actors to solve.

Furthermore, ICC officials insisted that the pursuit of peace and the pursuit of justice were separate endeavors and that it was outside the purview of the Court to affect peace. In a 2007 policy paper, the Office of the Prosecutor argued for a division of labor between the interests of justice and the interests of peace, maintaining that the former was the prerogative of the Court while the latter resided in the domain of

---

[66] International Crisis Group, "New ICC Prosecution: Opportunities and Risks for Peace in Sudan" (July 14, 2008).

[67] R. Green, *Controversy in the Arab World Over ICC Indictment of Sudan President Al-Bashir* (MEMRI Institute: 2008), p. 1.

[68] The Arab League, Egypt, and Syria supported the Sudanese government, maintaining that the ICC's intervention was "an American conspiracy." See Green, *Controversy in the Arab World*, p. 1. Sudan also looked to China and Russia for support. For a reaction by states and international organizations to the announcement that the Prosecutor was seeking an indictment, see A. Ciampi, "The Proceedings Against President Al Bashir and the Prospects of their Suspension under Article 16 ICC Statute" (2008) 6 *Journal of International Criminal Justice*, 5, pp. 885–897.

[69] African Union Peace and Security Council, "Communique of the 142nd Meeting of the Peace and Security Council" (July 21, 2008) AU Doc. PSC/MIN/Comm(CXLII).

[70] See "Mixed Reaction to Bashir Warrant," Al Jazeera, March 5, 2009.

[71] "Darfur and the ICC: Myths versus Reality," Human Rights Watch, March 27, 2009.

political actors such as the Security Council.[72] Judge Ekatarina Trendafilova also remarked that the ICC does not deal with "political issues" but only considers the law and the facts of a case, "and nothing else."[73] There is evidence, however, that suggests that Moreno-Ocampo was not ignorant of the political ramifications of his actions and that his decision-making may have been in part guided by political considerations and an interest in sequencing the ICC's intervention with efforts to establish peace.

First, while the Prosecutor was unapologetic in his zeal to indict Bashir, he could have applied for a sealed warrant rather than requesting a warrant for the President to be issued publicly. Rebecca Hamilton, who worked in the Office of the Prosecutor at the time, explained this decision:

> The issue was debated inside the Prosecutor's office. In the end the determination was made that it would be irresponsible if al-Bashir left Sudan one day and was extradited to The Hague the next without any prior warning to any of the internal or external actors involved in the daily business of the Sudanese state. The UN, AU, and the Sudanese people would wake up one morning to find al-Bashir gone and no transition plan would be in place. In contrast, signaling the intention to prosecute al-Bashir publicly and well in advance gave time for all the political actors to arrive at a consensus on the need for his arrest and to plan what the next steps would be following his extradition.[74]

Second, prior to requesting an indictment, Moreno-Ocampo publicly suggested that the ICC would take legal action if the atrocities in Darfur persisted. This was widely believed to be a public signal of intent to encourage Sudan to cooperate with the Court.[75]

Third, the Prosecutor was interested in sequencing his investigations in a politically sensitive manner. According to human rights lawyer Geoffrey Robertson, Moreno-Ocampo offered to delay any prosecution of Bashir in exchange for the surrender of Haroun to The Hague to be tried first.[76] This would allow the Court to test its evidence on a less senior figure before any prosecution of the President.

At the same time, opponents of the ICC's intervention, such as the AU, did not present a unanimous front. The AU's high-level panel headed by Thabo Mbeki, President of South Africa, indicated support for the ICC's case against Bashir.[77] Some senior ICC officials suggested that a number of African and Arab states agreed

[72]   ICC/OTP, "The Interest of Justice," Policy Paper on the Interests of Justice (September 2007).

[73]   E. Trendafilova, "Challenges before the International Criminal Court," lecture given at London School of Economics, November 26, 2009.

[74]   R. Hamilton, *Fighting for Darfur: Public Action and the Struggle to Stop Genocide* (New York: Palgrave Macmillan, 2011), p. 160.

[75]   Ibid.

[76]   G. Robertson, *Crimes Against Humanity – The Struggle for Global Justice* (London: Penguin, 2012), p. 556.

[77]   African Union Peace and Security Council, "Sudan: Communiqué of the 207th meeting of the Peace and Security Council" (October 29, 2009), AU Doc. PSC/AHG/COMM.1(CCVII).

that justice should be pursued against Bashir, but that they could not declare this publicly or officially.[78]

<h2 style="text-align:center">4.7 TIMING AND TRADING PEACE AND JUSTICE</h2>

Much of the debate over the wisdom of pursuing international criminal justice in Darfur pertains to timing. This underpinned the message offered by de Waal and Flint, who insisted that while international criminal justice is "a virtuous enterprise," pursuing it before achieving peace "spells disaster for Sudan."[79] Others, like Mahmoud Mamdani, have insisted that international responses to the conflict, including the ICC's intervention, have been characterized by a policy of acting first, thinking later.[80]

With arrest warrants already issued, concerted attention has been devoted to the possibility of halting the ICC's proceedings under Article 16 of the Rome Statute which permits the United Nations Security Council to defer any investigation or prosecution by the ICC for twelve months if it is deemed to be a threat to international peace and security.[81] The Council can renew such a deferral yearly.

Notably, Resolution 1593 included an explicit preamble reference to Article 16, suggesting that the UN Security Council viewed a potential deferral as a feasible means to balance peace and justice in Darfur.[82] As it became clear that Prosecutor Moreno-Ocampo was seeking an indictment for al-Bashir, the possibility of a deferral gained headway.

It is worth noting that Article 53 of the Rome Statute empowers the Prosecutor to reconsider a decision to initiate an investigation if he or she deems "a prosecution is not in the interest of justice ... "[83] This affords flexibility to the operations of the OTP at early stages of an investigation. However, as the Prosecutor furthers an investigation and the case moves before the Pre-Trial Chamber, opportunities for intervention by the OTP begin to narrow, raising the specter of UNSC deferral where states oppose ICC intervention.

Those actors that viewed the ICC's intervention as a potential risk to peace and security in Darfur openly supported a deferral. The AU threw its weight behind the move and, following the indictment of al-Bashir, they requested that the Security Council "defer the process initiated by the ICC, taking into account the need to ensure that the ongoing peace efforts are not jeopardized, as well as the fact that, in the current circumstances, a prosecution may not be in the interest of the victims and justice."[84] International NGOs also offered qualified support for a deferral. The

---

[78]   Confidential discussions with ICC officials.
[79]   J. Flint and A. de Waal, *Darfur – A New History of a Long War* (London: Zed Books, 2008).
[80]   Mamdani, *Saviors and Survivors.*   [81]   Rome Statute, Art. 16.   [82]   Security Council Res. 1593.
[83]   Rome Statute, Art. 53.
[84]   African Union Peace and Security Council, "AU's Peace and Security Council Resolution on Sudan President Indictment" (July 21, 2008).

International Crisis Group, headed at the time by Louise Arbour, the former Chief Prosecutor of the International Criminal Tribunals for the former Yugoslavia and Rwanda, stated that "the international community can help by offering incentives, provided Bashir and the NCP meet specific, irreversible benchmarks" that "would be necessary to end decades of chronic conflict – and perhaps save Sudan's unity." It would, therefore, be the exceptional situation for which Article 16 of the Rome Statute of the International Criminal Court was devised.[85] Even the United Kingdom and France, both ICC member states and Permanent Five Members of the Security Council, seemed open to a deferral if demonstrable gains in achieving peace were achieved.[86]

Others were concerned about the message a deferral would send Khartoum. HRW maintained that the situation did not warrant an Article 16 deferral because it did not pose a threat to international peace and security.[87] It also expressed concern over rewarding warring factions for retaliations against civilians and UN peacekeepers with deferral: "Yielding to intimidation of this kind would set a dangerous precedent and would make the international community susceptible to blackmail."[88] Geoffrey Robertson added that efforts to defer ICC action in Darfur were "encouraging Bashir to believe in his invincibility."[89] In a similar vein, Reeves expressed concern "that a deferral of the indictment would embolden the government."[90]

In the end, a resolution invoking Article 16 never reached the Security Council. The United States took a strong stance against any suspension of the Court's activities in Darfur, stating that it would veto any move to defer the case against al-Bashir. Publicly, US Special Envoy to Sudan Richard Williamson declared that "[w]e have not seen a response by the officials in Sudan to approach the sort of meaningful steps" regarding ongoing issues of peace, security, and humanitarian suffering.[91] Not wanting to table a resolution that would be vetoed, Security Council members decided against presenting the case for a deferral to the Council.[92]

4.8 CONSEQUENCES OF SIGNALING AND TIMING

Thus far, this case study has addressed the issue of timing in a two-fold manner. Historically, the diachronic analysis of state interests and geostrategic considerations

---

[85] International Crisis Group, "Sudan's Spreading Conflict (III): The Limits of Darfur's Peace Process" (January 27, 2014).

[86] A. de Waal, "Khartoum Should Not Count on an Article 16 Deferral of the ICC," African Arguments, September 18, 2008.

[87] "Article 16: Questions and Answers," Human Rights Watch, August 15, 2008.   [88] Ibid.

[89] Robertson, *Crimes Against Humanity*, p. 554.

[90] E. Reeves, "Darfur End Game: Peace or Justice in Sudan" *Sudan Tribune*, February 18, 2009.

[91] See D. Van Oudenaren, "US Will Veto Attempts to Defer ICC Move Against Sudan President: Official," *Sudan Tribune*, September 24, 2008.

[92] See Hamilton, *Fighting for Darfur*, pp. 161–162.

illustrates how the idea of referring Sudan to the ICC became possible and the process of persuading other UNSC members to support Resolution 1593 unfolded. In this regard, Bosco duly noted that "[t]he French and British campaign [for the referral of Sudan to the ICC] benefited from good timing."[93] Regarding the United States, the fact that the Bush administration had already used the term "genocide" to refer to the violence in Darfur helped greatly, as did the urgency to restore US moral leadership once human rights abuses committed in Iraq became public.[94]

Politically, the interactions between the ICC and Sudanese authorities show how the relationship between the parties (including cooperation from the latter) went from bad to worse. On the genesis of this bilateral relationship, exogenously-imposed ICC scrutiny on a non-party to the Rome Statute inevitably undercut the prospects of sincere cooperation from the Sudanese government from the onset. The already shaky relationship further deteriorated as the Prosecutor's office worked toward the identification, formal indictment, and apprehension of those allegedly responsible for the Darfur genocide. Sudanese aversion (and reaction) to the ICC grew stronger as judicial developments followed one another.

That said, the escalation of the Prosecutor's signaling strategy ultimately failed to bring about significant change in state behavior, let alone stopping Khartoum's genocidal plans. Vitriolic rhetoric notwithstanding, Sudanese reaction to OTP activities was mostly peaceful, at times even surprisingly cordial.[95] This gap between state rhetoric and behavior raises the issue of causality, for it entails that the independent variable(s) which can affect state behavior and thus deescalate genocidal violence is yet to be pinpointed.

If the cause of failure is exogenous to Sudan, a serious factor might be the lack of resolve shown by the international community since the day Resolution 1593 was adopted. From the outset, Resolution 1593 was weakened by restrictions on the obligations of non-states party to cooperate with the ICC, including broad exemptions for US military personnel, and the demand that funding for the investigation come exclusively from ICC member states. Put simply, Khartoum knew there was no collective resolve to coerce compliance with the ICC or enforce the arrest warrants, so it stood firm. In all, the international signaling strategy lacked consistency, and the fact that the OTP's internal strategy developed in accordance with signal theory precepts meant that it could not accomplish much by itself. That said, we must recognize the role of political actors and the UNSC in undermining the capacity of judicial actors to impart a strong signal.

In conclusion, it is worth noting that legal scholars and political scientists alike are paying increasing attention to the domestic politics of countries falling under ICC scrutiny, and the implications of their latest work may well be crucial for enhancing the ICC's impact across regions and countries. In particular, there is growing scholarly consensus on the autocratic rulers' tendency to exacerbate violence

---

[93] Bosco, *Rough Justice*, p. 109.   [94] Ibid., p. 110.   [95] Ibid., pp. 126, 144.

when cornered and conscious that they are about to lose power. Holding true the maxim that mechanisms of deterrence depend on the fact that individuals care about the future, the timing factor of the prosecutor's strategy may well make the difference between the deescalation and exacerbation of mass violence.

BIBLIOGRAPHY

Primary Sources

African Union High-Level Panel on Darfur (AUPD), "Communiqué of the Peace and Security Council 207th Meeting at the Level of the Heads of State and Government" (October 29, 2009), AU Doc. PSC/AHG/COMM.1(CCVII).

African Union Peace and Security Council, "Communiqué of the 142nd Meeting of the Peace and Security Council" (July 21, 2008) AU Doc. PSC/MIN/Comm(CXLII).

The Comprehensive Peace Agreement between The Government of The Republic of The Sudan and The Sudan People's Liberation Movement/Sudan People's Liberation Army, Naivasha, Kenya (December 31, 2004).

National Legislative Bodies/National Authorities, "Darfur Peace Agreement" (May 5, 2006).

Darfur Peace Document Draft, Sudan Tribune, April 27, 2011, available at www.sudantri bune.com/IMC/pdf/DPA-_Doha_draft.pdf

De la Sablière J.-M., "Darfur/ICC Statement by the French Ambassador De la Sablière After the Vote of Resolution 1593" (March 31, 2005).

EU–European Security and Defence Policy (ESDP), "EU Military Operation in Eastern Chad and North Eastern Central African Republic (EUFOR Tchad/RCA)" (updated March 2009), Tchad-RCA/9.

Human Rights Watch (HRW), "Article 16 – Questions and Answers," August 15, 2008, available at www.hrw.org/news/2008/08/15/q-article-16.

HRW, "Darfur and the ICC: Myths Versus Reality," March 27, 2009, available at www.hrw .org/news/2009/03/27/darfur-and-icc-myths-versus-reality.

HRW, "UN Security Council Refers Darfur to the ICC," April 1, 2005, available at www.hrw .org/news/2005/03/31/un-security-council-refers-darfur-icc.

International Criminal Court Press Release, "The Prosecutor of the ICC Opens Investigation in Darfur," June 6, 2005.

International Commission of Inquiry on Darfur, "Report of the International Commission of Inquiry on Darfur to the United Nations Secretary-General" (January 25, 2005).

Jackson R. H., "The Federal Prosecutor," April 1, 1940, Speech.

ICC/OTP, "The Interest of Justice," Policy Paper on the Interests of Justice (September 2007).

The Prosecutor V. Abdallah Banda Abakaer Nourain, Warrant of Arrest for Abdallah Banda Abakaer Nourain [2014] ICC-02/05–03/09.

The Prosecutor v. Ahmad Muhammad Harun ("Ahmad Harun") and Ali Muhammad Al Abd-Al-Rahman ("Ali Kushayb"), Warrant of Arrest for Ahmad Harun [2007] ICC-02/05–01/07.

The Prosecutor v. Bahar Idriss Abu Garda, Decision on Confirmation of Charges [2010] ICC-02/05–02/09.

The Prosecutor v. Omar Hassan Ahmad Al Bashir, Decision on the Cooperation of the Democratic Republic of the Congo Regarding Omar Al Bashir's Arrest and Surrender to the Court [2014] ICC-02/05–01/09.

The Prosecutor v. Omar Hassan Ahmad Al Bashir, Decision informing the United Nations Security Council and the Assembly of the States Parties to the Rome Statute about Omar Al-Bashir's presence in the territory of the Republic of Kenya [2010] ICC-02/05–01/09.

The Prosecutor v. Omar Hassan Ahmad Al Bashir, Decision on the Non-Compliance of the Republic of Chad with the Cooperation Requests Issued by the Court Regarding the Arrest and Surrender of Omar Hassan Ahmad Al-Bashir [2013] ICC-02/05–01/09.

The Prosecutor v. Omar Hassan Ahmad Al Bashir, Decision on the Prosecutor's Request for a Finding of Non-Compliance Against the Republic of Sudan [2015] ICC-02/05–01/09.

The Prosecutor v. Omar Hassan Ahmad Al Bashir, Judgment on the Appeal of the Prosecutor against the "Decision on the Prosecution's Application for a Warrant of Arrest against Omar Hassan Ahmad Al Bashir" [2010] ICC-02/05–01/09-OA.

The Prosecutor v. Omar Hassan Ahmad Al Bashir, Second Warrant of Arrest for Omar Hassan Ahmad Al Bashir [2010] ICC-02/05–01/09.

The Prosecutor v. Omar Hassan Ahmad Al Bashir, Warrant of Arrest for Omar Hassan Ahmad Al Bashir [2009] ICC-02/05–01/09.

Rome Statute of the International Criminal Court, Rome, July 17, 1998, in force July 1 2002, 2187 UNTS 38544.

Séance Publique du Conseil de Sécurité (March 31, 2005), available at www.iccnow.org/documents/France.Statement.SCreferralDarfurICC_31March05.pdf

Trendafilova E., "Challenges Before the International Criminal Court," Lecture at London School of Economics, November 26, 2009.

United Nations (UN) News Center, "Security Council Inaction on Darfur 'Can Only Embolden Perpetrators' – ICC Prosecutor," December 12, 2014.

UN Press Release, "Secretary-General's Speech to the 54th Session of the General Assembly," September 20, 1999.

UN Press Release, "Security Council Refers Situation in Darfur, Sudan, to Prosecutor of International Criminal Court," March 31, 2005.

UN Security Council (UNSC), Resolution 1564 (September 18, 2004), UN Doc. S/RES/1564.

UNSC, Resolution 1593 (March 31, 2005), UN Doc. S/RES/1593.

UNSC, Resolution 1769 (July 31, 2007), UN Doc. S/RES/1769.

UNSC, Resolution 1970 (February 26, 2011), UN Doc. S/RES/1970.

UNSC, "Full Draft: UN Resolution Referring Syria to the ICC" (May 22, 2014) UN Doc. S/2014/348.

US Department of State Archive, "American Service-Members' Protection Act," July 30, 2003, available at http://2001–2009.state.gov/t/pm/rls/othr/misc/23425.htm.

US Department of State Archive, "International Criminal Court: Letter to UN Secretary-General Kofi Annan," May 6, 2002.

US Department of State Archive, "The Crisis in Darfur – Testimony before the Senate Foreign Relations Committee by Secretary Colin L. Powell," September 9, 2004.

Secondary Sources

Books

Allen T., *Trial Justice: The International Criminal Court and the Lord's Resistance Army* (London: Zed Books, 2006).

Bosco D., *"Rough Justice – The International Criminal Court in a World of Power Politics"* (Oxford: Oxford University Press, 2014).

Cassese A., *International Criminal Law*, 2nd Edition (New York: Oxford University Press, 2008).

Crilly R., *Saving Darfur – Everyone's Favourite African War* (UK: Reportage Press, 2010).

De la Sablière J.-M., *Dans les Coulisses du Monde: Du Rwanda à la Guerre d'Irak, un Grand Négociateur Révèle le Dessous des Cartes* (Paris: Editions Robert Lafront, 2013).

De la Sablière J.-M., *Le Conseil de Sécurité des Nations Unies: Ambitions et Limites* (Bruxelles: Editions Larcier, 2015).

Dorman A. M., *Blair's Successful War: British Military Intervention in Sierra Leone* (Ashgate Publishing, Ltd., 2009).

Flint J. and de Waal A., *Darfur – A New History of a Long War* (London: Zed Books, 2008).

Glasius M., *The International Criminal Court – A Global Civil Society Achievement* (London: Routledge, 2006).

Grono N. and O'Brien A., "Justice in Conflict? The ICC and Peace Processes" in Waddell N. and Clark P. (eds.) *Courting Conflict? Justice, Peace and the ICC in Africa* (London: Royal African Society, 2008).

Hagan J., *Justice in the Balkans: Prosecuting War Crimes in the Hague Tribunal* (University of Chicago Press, 2003).

Hagan J. and Rymond-Richmond W., *Darfur and the Crime of Genocide* (Cambridge: Cambridge University Press, 2009).

Hamilton R., *Fighting for Darfur: Public Action and the Struggle to Stop Genocide* (New York: Palgrave Macmillan, 2011).

Mamdani M., *Saviors and Survivors: Darfur, Politics, and the War on Terror* (New York City: Doubleday, 2009).

Nathan A. J. and Scobell A., *China's Search for Security* (New York: Columbia University Press, 2012).

Neier A., *War Crimes* (New York: Times Books, 1998).

Nouwen S. M. H., *Complementarity in the Line of Fire – The Catalysing Effect of the International Criminal Court in Uganda and Sudan* (Cambridge: Cambridge University Press, 2013).

Reeves E., *A Long Day's Dying: Critical Moments in the Darfur Genocide* (Toronto: The Key Publishing House Incorporated, 2007).

Robertson G., *Crimes Against Humanity – The Struggle for Global Justice* (London: Penguin, 2012).

Schabas W., *An Introduction to the International Criminal Court* (Cambridge: Cambridge University Press, 2007).

Schiff B., *Building the International Criminal Court* (Cambridge: Cambridge University Press, 2008).

Shambaugh D. L., *China Goes Global: The Partial Power* (Oxford University Press, 2013).

Shirk S. L, *China: Fragile Superpower* (Oxford University Press, 2008).

Sikkink K., *The Justice Cascade: How Human Rights Prosecutions Are Changing World Politics* (New York: W.W. Norton & Company, 2011).

Waal A., "Darfur, the Court and Khartoum: The Politics of State Non-Cooperation" in Waddell N. and Clark P. (eds.), *Courting Conflict? Justice, Peace and the ICC in Africa* (London: Royal African Society, 2008).

Weinstein J. M., *Inside Rebellion: The Politics of Insurgent Violence* (Cambridge University Press, 2006).

Articles and Reports

Akhavan P., "The Crime of Genocide in the ICTR Jurisprudence" (2005) 3 *Journal of International Criminal Justice*, 4, pp. 989–1006.

Akhavan P., "Are International Criminal Tribunals a Disincentive to Peace?: Reconciling Judicial Romanticism with Political Realism" (2009) 31 *Human Rights Quarterly*, 31, pp. 624–654.

Alexander J. F., "The International Criminal Court and the Prevention of Atrocities: Predicting the Court's Impact" (2009) 54 *Villanova Law Review* 1, pp. 1–56.

Annan K., "Two Concepts of Sovereignty," *The Economist*, September 18, 1999, pp. 49–50.

Bocchese M., "Coercing Compliance with the ICC: Empirical Assessment and Theoretical Implications" (2015) 24 *Michigan State International Law Review*, 357.

Bosco D., "The International Criminal Court and Crime Prevention: Byproduct or Conscious Goal" (2010) 19 *Michigan State Journal of International Law*, 2, pp. 163–200.

Burke-White W. W., "Complementarity in Practice: The International Criminal Court as Part of a System of Multi-level Global Governance in the Democratic Republic of Congo" (2005) 18 *Leiden Journal of International Law*, 3, pp. 557–590.

Ciampi A., "The Proceedings Against President Al Bashir and the Prospects of their Suspension under Article 16 ICC Statute" (2008) 6 *Journal of International Criminal Justice*, 5, pp. 885–897.

Clark P., "If Ocampo Indicts Bashir, Nothing May Happen," African Arguments, July 13, 2008.

"Conflict in Sudan's Darfur Displaces 41,000 in Two Months: UN," Yahoo! News, February 19, 2015.

Corell H., "Challenges for the International Criminal Court" (2014) *International Judicial Monitor Winter* (2014), available at: www.judicialmonitor.org/archive_winter2014/specialreport1.html

Corell H., "Commentary: International Prosecution of Heads of State for Genocide, War Crimes, and Crimes against Humanity" (2009) 43 *The John Marshall Law Review* XXV, pp. xxv–xli.

Cronin-Furman K., "Managing Expectations: International Criminal Trials and the Prospects for Deterrence of Mass Atrocity" (2013) 7 *International Journal of Transitional Justice*, 3, pp. 434–454.

Cryer R., "Sudan, Resolution 1593 and International Criminal Justice" (2006) 19 *Leiden Journal of International Law*, pp. 195–222.

De Waal, A., "Khartoum Should Not Count On an Article 16 Deferral of the ICC," African Arguments, September 18, 2008.

Escribà-Folch A. and Wright J., "Human Rights Prosecutions and Autocratic Survival" (2015) 69 *International Organization*, 2, pp. 343–373.

Fearon J. D., "Signaling Foreign Policy Interests – Tying Hands Versus Sinking Costs" (1997) 41 *Journal of Conflict Resolution*, 1, pp. 68–90.

Flint J. and de Waal A., "Justice Off Course in Darfur," *The Washington Post*, June 28, 2008.

Flint J. and de Waal A., "To Put Justice Before Peace Spells Disaster for Sudan," *The Guardian*, March 6, 2009.

Geis J. and Mundt A., "When to Indict? The Impact of Timing of International Criminal Indictments on Peace Processes and Humanitarian Action," Brookings Report for the World Humanitarian Studies Conference (February 2009), p. 1.

Green R., "Controversy in the Arab World Over ICC Indictment of Sudan President Al-Bashir," The Middle East Media Research Institute, July 24, 2008.

Harper M., "What if Ocampo Indicts Bashir?" African Arguments, June 17, 2008.

"ICC Prosecutor Shelves Darfur War Crimes Inquiries," BBC News, December 12, 2014.

International Crisis Group (ICG), "Sudan's Spreading Conflict (III): The Limits of Darfur's Peace Process" (January 27, 2014).

Jervis R., "Rational Deterrence: Theory and Evidence" (1989) 41 *World Politics*, 2, pp. 183–207.

Keller L. M., "Achieving Peace with Justice: The International Criminal Court and Ugandan Alternative Justice Mechanisms" (2007) 23 *Connecticut Journal of International Law*, pp. 209–279.

Kelley J., "Who Keeps International Commitments and Why? The International Criminal Court and Bilateral Nonsurrender Agreements" (2007) 101 *American Political Science Review*, 3, pp. 573–589.

Kersten M., "Full Draft: UN Resolution Referring Syria to the ICC, Justice in Conflict," Justice in Conflict, May 12, 2014.

Kim H. and Sikkink K., "Explaining the Deterrence Effect of Human Rights Prosecutions for Transitional Countries" (2010) 54 *International Studies Quarterly*, 4, pp. 939–963.

Ku J. and Nzelibe J., "Do International Criminal Tribunals Deter or Exacerbate Humanitarian Atrocities" (2006) 84 *Washington University Law Review*, 4, pp. 777–833.

Kurth J., "Humanitarian Intervention after Iraq: Legal Ideals vs. Military Realities" (2007) 50 *Orbis*, 1, pp. 87–101.

Lee M. R., "UN Says Flying ICC Indictee Haroun Was in its Budget, Won't Disclose Cost" Inner City Press, 2011.

Lesnes C., "A l'ONU la Discussion sur le Jugement des Crimes Commis au Dafur Continue," *Le Monde*, March 25, 2005.

Lynch C., "Sudan's Omar al-Bashir Cancels UN Trip, Foreign Policy," Foreign Policy, September 25, 2013.

"Mixed Reaction to Bashir Warrant," Al Jazeera Media Network, March 5, 2009.

"New ICC Prosecution: Opportunities and Risks for Peace in Sudan," Reliefweb, July 14, 2008.

Majzub D., "Peace or Justice-Amnesties and the International Criminal Court" (2002) 3 *Melbourne Journal of International Law*, pp. 247–279.

McDonald A., "Sierra Leone's Shoestring Special Court" (2002) 84 *International Review of the Red Cross*, 845, pp. 121–143.

Meernik J., "Justice and Peace? How the International Criminal Tribunal Affects Societal Peace in Bosnia" (2005) 42 *Journal of Peace Research*, 3, pp. 271–289.

Mehler A., "Peace and Power Sharing in Africa: A Not so Obvious Relationship" (2009) 108 *African Affairs*, 432, 453–473.

Mehler A., "Rebels and Parties: The Impact of Armed Insurgency on Representation in the Central African Republic" (2011) 49 *The Journal of Modern African Studies*, 1, pp. 115–139.

Melly P. and Darracq V., "A New Way to Engage? French Policy in Africa from Sarkozy to Hollande" Chatham House Africa 2013/01 (May 2013).

Nmoma V., "The Shift in United States–Sudan Relations: A Troubled Relationship and the Need for Mutual Cooperation" (2006) 26 *Journal of Conflict Studies* 2, pp. 44–70.

Polgreen L. and Simons M., "The Pursuit of Justice vs. the Pursuit of Peace," *The New York Times*, July 11, 2008.

"Powell Declares Genocide in Sudan," BBC News, September 9, 2004.

Punyasena W., "Conflict Prevention and the International Criminal Court: Deterrence in a Changing World" (2006) 14 *Michigan State Journal of International Law*, pp. 39–70.

Reeves E., "Darfur End Game: Peace or Justice in Sudan," Sudan Reeves, 2009.

Reeves E., "Turning up the Heat in Darfur," *The Guardian*, July 17, 2008.

Rodman K. A. and Booth P., "Manipulated Commitments: The International Criminal Court in Uganda" (2013) 35 *Human Rights Quarterly*, 2, pp. 271–303.

Rodriguez P. M., "UNSC: Darfur's Referral Turns 10 Years," Huffington Post HPMG News, March 9 2015.

Scheffer D. et al., "The Collective International Responsibility to Protect: The Case of Darfur, Reforming the United Nations: The Use of Force to Safeguard International Security and Human Rights" (2005) 4 *Northwestern University Journal of International Human Rights*, 1, pp. 118–137.

Scheffer D., "Article 98(2) of the Rome Statute: America's Original Intent" (2005) 3 *Journal of International Criminal Justice*, 2, pp. 333–353.

Scheffer D., "The Unbearable Constancy of Atrocity Crimes in Darfur and the Eastern Congo" (2007) 5 *Northwestern University Journal of International Human Rights*, 3, pp. 322–325.

Sengupta S., "Sudan Joins Coalition Against Yemen Rebels," *The New York Times*, March 26, 2015.

Snyder J. and Vinjamuri L., "Trials and Errors: Principles and Pragmatism in Strategies of International Justice" (2003–2004) 28 *International Security*, 3, pp. 5–44.

Stanton G. H., "Could the Rwandan Genocide have been Prevented?" (2004) 6 *Journal of Genocide Research*, 2, pp. 211–228.

Straus S., "Darfur and the Genocide Debate" (2005) 84 *Foreign Affairs*, 1, pp. 123–133.

"UN: 460,000 Displaced in Darfur this Year," Al Jazeera Media Network, November 4, 2013.

Simons M., "Without Fanfare or Cases, International Court Sets Up," *The New York Times*, July 1, 2002.

"The Security Council's Struggle over Darfur and International Justice," JURIST, August 20, 2008.

"United Nations and Darfur – Fact Sheet" (2007), available at www.un.org/news/dh/infocus/sudan/fact_sheet.pdf.

Van Oudenaren D., "US Will Veto Attempts to Defer ICC Move Against Sudan President: Official," *Sudan Tribune*, September 24, 2008.

Villa-Vicencio C., "Why Perpetrators Should Not Always Be Prosecuted: Where the International Criminal Court and Truth Commissions Meet" (2000) 49 *Emory Law Journal*, pp. 205–222.

Vinjamuri L., "Deterrence, Democracy, and the Pursuit of International Justice" (2010) 2 *Ethics & International Affairs*, 2, pp. 191–211.

De Waal, A., "ICC, Dangers Weeks Ahead, Social Science Research Council," African Arguments, 2009.

Weisman S. R., "US Rethinks its Cutoff of Military Aid to Latin American Nations," *The New York Times*, March 12, 2006.

Williams P., "Fighting for Freetown: British Military Intervention in Sierra Leone" (2001) 22 *Contemporary Security Policy*, 3, pp. 140–168.

5

Alignment

Identifying Potential Alignments Between Diplomatic and Judicial Processes

FOCUS: LIBYA

Executive summary: This case study examines the tensions that arose between parallel – and sometimes competing – diplomatic and judicial processes during the 2011 humanitarian crisis in Libya. Muammar Gaddafi, the country's long-ruling dictator, deployed military force to suppress protestors who, buoyed by the Arab Spring, demanded his ouster. Efforts to address short-term imperatives of protecting civilians and longer-term goals of holding Gaddafi and other perpetrators accountable underscored the complex relationship between peace and justice within the framework of international law.

On February 26, 2011, the UN Security Council passed Resolution 1970, referring the crisis in Libya to the Office of the Prosecutor (OTP) at the International Criminal Court (ICC) in The Hague, and providing for embargoes, sanctions and other assertive measures to end the conflict. Less than three weeks later, the UNSC authorized military intervention under Chapter VII of the UN Charter, extending the embargo and asset freezes, while acknowledging the concurrent judicial actions by the ICC. The ICC Prosecutor saw these resolutions as an opportunity to "hitch international justice to military power" and initiated a prompt and aggressive investigation.[1] But diplomatic support for the ICC was undermined by the shifted focus on military action and diplomatic efforts to negotiate "an arrangement" for Gaddafi to relinquish power in exchange for immunity from prosecution. However, international engagement in Libya diminished sharply following the fall of the Gaddafi regime leaving the new authorities confronted by militias and terrorist groups and abandoning any follow-up of ICC indictments. The contradictory actions underscore the need for diplomats to understand the full implications of a Security Council referral to the ICC.

---

[1] D. Bosco, "Cool Ties," *Foreign Policy*, February 28, 2014.

This case raises several questions: What motivated the UNSC to act in referring the Libya case to the ICC at the time the National Transitional Council was created? To what extent were considerations of conflict resolution weighed in conjunction with the imperatives of international criminal justice? Could the contradictions between two UN-mandated processes have been reframed as assets in negotiation processes? Are there existing processes or mechanisms that could permit better coordination? If not, what might they be?

5.1 BACKGROUND

5.1.1 *Libya, the 2011 Civil War and the UN Security Council*

In the early weeks of 2011, Libyans took to the streets in protest of the forty-year rule of Muammar Gaddafi. Emboldened by the "Arab Spring" spreading across the region, citizens demanded change. In its initial phases, the Libyan uprising was not explicitly about removing Gaddafi from power. Rather, it was fueled by demands for genuine socio-economic and political reforms. This quickly changed as security forces from the Gaddafi regime reacted to largely peaceful protests with overwhelming force, going so far as to target civilians attending funerals of fallen compatriots. By the end of February 2011, it had become increasingly clear that the regime would readily employ violence to suppress the rising protests. Gaddafi infamously declared that state forces would go "street to street, alley to alley" to "cleanse" Libya of anyone opposing his rule.[2] He also encouraged his supporters to attack the "cockroaches" rising up against the regime.[3] The situation in Libya descended into a civil war that pitted the regime against a diverse collective of rebel factions and their political wing, the National Transitional Council (NTC).[4] The motivation of opposition forces also markedly changed as they embraced the goal of removing the regime, a goal later shared and reinforced by the NATO-led military intervention.

The Gaddafi regime's response to the uprising galvanized broad international, regional, and local condemnation of the violence.[5] Defectors from the Libyan mission to the United Nations made an impassioned plea to the international community to take action in order to stop what they viewed as a potential "genocide"

---

[2] "What Qaddafi Said," *Foreign Affairs*, June 4, 2011.

[3] "Libya Protests: Defiant Qaddafi Refuses to Quit," BBC News, February 22, 2011.

[4] The creation of the NTC was announced on February 26, 2011, to serve as the political face of the rebellion and as an umbrella organization under which various opposition factions could coalesce against the Gaddafi regime. Ex-Minister of Justice Mustafa Mohamed Abdu Ajleil was the primary driver behind the creation of the NTC. The NTC leadership comprised defectors from the Gaddafi regime, activists, and lawyers, among others. The NTC governed for a period of nine months between 2011 and 2012, when power was officially transferred to the General National Congress.

[5] See S. Chesterman, "Leading from Behind: The Responsibility to Protect, The Obama Doctrine, and Humanitarian Intervention After Libya" (2011) 25 *Ethics & International Affairs*, 3, p.4.

in Libya. On February 21, Ibrahim Dabbashi, Libyan's Deputy Ambassador to the UN, declared:

> Gaddafi's regime has already started the genocide against the Libyan people since January 15. His soldiers and the mercenaries being flown into the country were ordered to shoot to kill ... We call on the UN Security Council to use the principle of the right to protect to take the necessary action to protect the Libyan people against the genocide ... We also call on the Prosecutor of the International Criminal Court to start immediately investigating the crimes committed by Gaddafi.[6]

The Organization of the Islamic Conference, the Arab League, and the African Union all issued statements condemning the regime's crackdown on peaceful protests.[7] Mindful of such declarations, on February 26, the UN Security Council unanimously passed Resolution 1970. The resolution imposed a package of sanctions, as well as a travel ban and asset freeze against the regime and members of the Gaddafi family. Notably, it also referred the situation in Libya to the ICC for investigation.[8] The speed with which the UNSC passed resolution 1970 was likely due – at least in part – to this broad condemnation of violence by Arab and African states. The Libyan representative to the UNSC likewise condemned the Gaddafi regime and expressed his support for international intervention.[9] Under these circumstances, it would have been politically untenable for UNSC member states to oppose intervention behind a veil of non-interference.

As the violence escalated and civilian casualties increased, a diverse coalition of actors pressed for intervention. Both the OIC and the Arab League issued statements supporting international action to enforce a no-fly zone over Libya.[10] On March 17 – less than a month following the passage of resolution 1970 – the Security

---

[6] See M. du Plessis and A. Louw, "Justice and the Libyan Crisis: The ICC's Role under Security Council Resolution 1970" (2011) *Institute for Security Studies Briefing Paper*, pp. 1–2, "UN Ambassador Dabbashi, Letter Dated February 21, 2011 from the Chargé d'affaires a.i. of the Permanent Mission of the Libyan Arab Jamahiriya to the United Nations Addressed to the President of the Security Council" (February 21, 2011) UN Doc. S/2011/102.

[7] On February 22, the Arab League suspended Libyan participation in meetings of the governing council. See O. Galal, "Arab League Bars Libya From Meetings, Citing Forces' 'Crimes,'" Bloomberg, February 2, 2011. See also African Union Peace and Security Council, "Communique of the 261th Meeting of the Peace and Security Council" (February 23, 2011) AU Doc. PSC/PR/ COMM (CCLXI); "OIC General Secretariat Condemns Strongly the Excessive Use of Force against Civilians in the Libyan Jamahiriya," OIC Press Release, February 22, 2011.

[8] Security Council Res. 1970 (February 26, 2011), UN Doc. S/RES/1970.

[9] "In Swift, Decisive Action, Security Council Imposes Tough Measures on Libyan Regime, Adopting Resolution 1970 in Wake of Crackdown on Protesters," Security Council Meetings Coverage, February 26, 2011.

[10] See "The Outcome of the Council of the League of Arab States meeting at the Ministerial level in its extraordinary session on the implications of the current events in Libya and the Arab position," Cairo, March 12, 2011.

Council adopted Resolution 1973, authorizing member states to take "all necessary measures" to protect civilians by enforcing a no-fly zone over Libya.[11] Thirty-seven states joined the coalition of the willing to enforce Resolution 1973, including the United States, the United Kingdom, and members of the Arab League and OIC. Following a March 27 meeting in Brussels, NATO agreed to spearhead command of military operations.

5.2 RESOLUTION 1970 AND THE ICC

Within two weeks of the UNSC referral via Resolution 1970, ICC Chief Prosecutor Luis Moreno-Ocampo opened an official investigation into alleged crimes committed in Libya. On May 16, 2011, the Prosecutor requested that the Court issue arrest warrants for three alleged perpetrators: leader Muammar Gaddafi; Abdullah al-Senussi, Libya's head of internal and military intelligence; and Saif al-Islam Gaddafi, son of the Libyan leader and one-time heir apparent.[12] On June 27, the ICC's Pre-Trial Chamber issued warrants for all three.[13]

The turnaround time from receiving a referral to issuing an arrest warrant was unprecedented. In Darfur, the only other case of a UN Security Council referral to the ICC, the Court took two years to move from accepting the referral to issuing arrest warrants. In Libya, it took a matter of weeks. The speed of decision-making within the Office of the Prosecutor can be explained in part by the OTP's eagerness to capture the interest of an international community seemingly eager to support the Prosecutor's work. In other words, the ICC Prosecutor viewed the Security Council referral as an opportunity to demonstrate the utility of the Court, and he may have seized the political and legal opening to foreclose the possibility of an immunity deal.[14]

To be sure, there was reason to suspect that a political settlement might be struck allowing Gaddafi to stay in Libya. Shortly after the arrest warrants were issued, the British Foreign Secretary, William Hague, suggested that Gaddafi might stay in Libya

---

[11] The resolution was unanimously adopted. Ten Council members voted for the resolution (Bosnia and Herzegovina, Colombia, France, Gabon, Lebanon, Nigeria, Portugal, South Africa, the UK and the USA) and five abstained (Brazil, China, Germany, India and Russia). While military force was authorized, the resolution excluded the use of a foreign occupying force, mirroring the demands of earlier Libyan and Arab League requests. See Security Council Res. 1973 (March 17, 2011), UN Doc. S/RES/1973.

[12] *Situation in the Libyan Arab Jamahiriya*, Prosecutor's Application Pursuant to Article 58 as to Muammar Mohammed Abu Minyar Gaddafi, Saif Al-Islam Gaddafi and Abdullah Al-Senussi [2011] ICC-01/11-4-Red.

[13] See *Situation in the Libyan Arab Jamahiriya*, Warrant of Arrest for Abdullah Al-Senussi [2011] ICC-01/11-15; *Situation in the Libyan Arab Jamahiriya*, Warrant of Arrest for Saif Al-Islam Qaddafi [2011] ICC-01/11-14; and *Situation in the Libyan Arab Jamahiriya*, Warrant of Arrest for Muammar Mohammed Abu Minyar Gaddafi [2011] ICC-01/11-13.

[14] See M. Kersten, "Justice in Conflict: The ICC in Libya and Northern Uganda," PhD thesis, London School of Economics (2014); M. Kersten, *Justice in Conflict: The Effects of the International Criminal Court's Interventions on Ending Wars and Building Peace* (Oxford: Oxford University Press, 2016).

if he agreed to step down from power. This proposition echoed a similar statement by the Libyan opposition National Transitional Council.[15] However, an ICC spokesperson responded in a public statement that the indictment was a "legal fact" with no other available options. "He has to be arrested," the spokesperson said.[16]

In addition to regime officials, there have also been calls for the ICC to prosecute crimes allegedly perpetrated by rebels during the civil war. In 2012, the International Commission of Inquiry on Libya, established by the UN Human Rights Council the previous year, concluded that "war crimes and crimes against humanity were committed by rebels, or *thuwar*, and that breaches of international human rights law continue to occur in a climate of impunity."[17] Numerous observers decried the forced expulsion of the city of Tawergha by the Misratan rebels in an act of apparent retaliation for supporting the Gaddafi regime. Kevin Jon Heller has argued that "[i]t is at least arguable that the Misratan *thuwar* committed genocide against the Tawerghans."[18] His argument is supported by evidence, cited in the International Commission of Inquiry on Libya's report of March 2012, that the Misratan rebels declared that Tawergha deserved "to be wiped off the face of the planet."[19] The Commission added that "[t]he Misrata *thuwar* have killed, arbitrarily arrested and tortured Tawerghans across Libya."[20]

Ultimately, the Libyan opposition, bolstered by the intervention of NATO-led forces, achieved its goal of regime change. In October 2011, opposition forces captured and killed Muammar Gaddafi. The violent circumstances surrounding the death of the former Libyan leader led to calls for further scrutiny by the ICC.[21] The OTP has maintained that it continues to "collect information" on allegations of rape and sexual violence, as well as crimes by rebel or revolutionary fighters.[22] Despite these allegations, the ICC has yet to issue more indictments in the Libyan case.

5.3 ADMISSIBILITY CHALLENGE AND COMPLEMENTARITY

Under the Rome Statute, states have the right to challenge the admissibility of cases brought before the ICC.[23] While the ICC retains the authority to determine whether

---

[15] R. Norton-Taylor and C. Stephen, "Qaddafi Can't be Left in Libya, Says International Criminal Court," *The Guardian*, July 26, 2011.

[16] Ibid.

[17] Human Rights Council, "Report of the International Commission of Inquiry on Libya" (March 2, 2012), UN Doc. A/HRC/19/68.

[18] K. J. Heller, "The International Commission of Inquiry on Libya: A Critical Analysis," in J. Meierhenrich (ed.), *International Commissions: The Role of Commissions of Inquiry in the Investigation of International Crimes* (forthcoming).

[19] "Report of the International Commission of Inquiry on Libya." [20] Ibid.

[21] See "Qaddafi's Death may be War Crime: ICC Prosecutor," Reuters, December 16, 2011.

[22] "International Criminal Court Prosecutor Calls on Libyan Authorities to Ensure no Impunity," UN News Service, November 7, 2012.

[23] Rome Statute of the International Criminal Court, Rome, July 17, 1998, in force July 1, 2002, 2187 UNTS 38544, Art. 19(2).

it has the jurisdiction to try a case, a challenge may be raised if, for example, a state with jurisdiction claims it is investigating and prosecuting the case.[24] As Mark Ellis notes, even a state that is not party to the Rome Statute, such as Libya, may exercise the right to challenge admissibility in the case of a referral by the UN Security Council.[25] The UNSC referral imposes the same obligations as for States Parties and therefore entitles the referee government to challenge admissibility under the principle of complementarity.

After a preliminary examination of the available evidence surrounding the charges against Saif al-Islam Gaddafi and Abdullah al-Senussi, ICC Prosecutor Luis Moreno-Ocampo concluded that there was no "genuine national investigation or prosecution" taking place to satisfy the criteria for deference to national authorities.[26] Libyan officials, for their part, argued that the trials of Gaddafi and Senussi were of national importance and should be conducted in Libya.

In May 2012, the government in Tripoli formally challenged the admissibility of the ICC's case against Gaddafi.[27] Libya asserted that it was actively investigating Gaddafi for the same crimes as the ones before the ICC and, moreover, that it was willing and able to prosecute the case in domestic courts.[28] ICC Pre-Trial Chamber I heard oral arguments regarding the nature of the Libyan investigation, including methods of evidence gathering, the legal basis for monitoring domestic cases, and the application of procedural rights to Gaddafi's case.[29] While Libya maintained it was capable of prosecuting the Gaddafi case, the OTP argued that Libya had not adequately demonstrated it was competently investigating the same charges as those before the ICC. Notably, the UN International Commission of Inquiry in Libya reported that "few officials demonstrate 'a real understanding of basic legal and human rights standards.'"[30] The Offices of Public Council for the Victims and for the Defense both similarly called for the ICC to reject the challenge. On May 31, 2013, the Pre-Trial Chamber rejected the challenge and ruled that Saif's case was admissible before the Court given that Libya was unable to prosecute Saif as long as he remained outside the custody of the central authorities:

> [T]he Chamber is of the view that its national system cannot yet be applied in full in areas or aspects relevant to the case, being thus "unavailable" within the terms of article 17(3) of the Statute. As a consequence, Libya is "unable to obtain the accused" and the necessary testimony and is also "otherwise unable to carry out

---

[24]   Ibid., Art. 19(2)(b).

[25]   M. S. Ellis, *Sovereignty and Justice: Balancing the Principle of Complementarity between International and Domestic War Crimes Tribunals* (Cambridge Scholars Publishing, 2014), p. 198.

[26]   ICC/OTP, "Report on Preliminary Examination Activities" (December 13, 2011), para. 118 as discussed in Ellis, *Sovereignty and Justice*, pp. 200–201.

[27]   In January 2012, the NTC had initiated investigations into crimes of rape and murder allegedly perpetrated by Saif Al-Islam Gaddafi. See Ellis, *Sovereignty and Justice*, p. 200.

[28]   See *The Prosecutor v. Saif Al-Islam Gaddafi and Abdullah Al-Senussi*, Application on Behalf of the Government of Libya Pursuant to Article 19 of the Rome Statute [2012] ICC-01/11–01/11–130-Red, p. 3.

[29]   Ellis, *Sovereignty and Justice*, p. 208.   [30]   Ibid., p. 209.

[the] proceedings" in the case against Mr. Gaddafi in compliance with its national laws, in accordance with the same provision.[31]

As of this writing, Saif has been convicted of war crimes in absentia and sentenced to death by a Libyan court, though he remains in the custody of rebel forces in Zintan.[32]

Conversely, in the case of Al-Senussi, both the Libyan government and the OTP asked the Pre-Trial Chamber to declare the case inadmissible before the international court. Al-Senussi was surrendered to Libyan authorities after being detained in Mauritania in September 2012. Libyan officials subsequently initiated criminal proceedings against the former intelligence chief. Upon review, ICC Pre-Trial Chamber I determined that competent domestic authorities in Libya were conducting domestic proceedings against al-Senussi, and that Libya was neither unwilling nor unable to fulfill its responsibilities vis-à-vis international law.[33] As such, the Pre-Trial Chamber ruled the case against al-Senussi inadmissible before the ICC.[34] While the ruling ostensibly defers to the complementarity principle, it curiously centers on the "ability" of Libya to carry out a domestic investigation against Al-Senussi rather than the actual procedural irregularities that had already taken place, such as problems with due process.[35] In other words, the procedural barriers the Court recognized as problematic in the Gaddafi case, which led it to conclude that a domestic trial would not meet international standards, seemed to be afforded less weight in the Al-Senussi case.[36]

Furthermore, the Court's willingness to monitor the domestic investigation in the Al-Senussi case points to a tension with the Court's more explicit rejection of Libya's ability to try Gaddafi. These divergent outcomes point to the Court's uncertainty about its own role in monitoring the domestic investigations and justice outcomes called for in UNSC Resolution 1970, and to what extent complementarity allows for or even requires follow-up by the ICC.

5.4 RESOLUTION 1970 – POLITICAL CONSTRAINTS ON JUSTICE[37]

The decision by the UN Security Council to refer the Libya case to the ICC underscored the importance of timing and the broader strategic interests of member

---

[31]   *The Prosecutor v. Saif Al-Islam Gaddafi and Abdullah Al-Senussi*, Decision on the Admissibility of the Case Against Saif Al-Islam Gaddafi [2013] ICC-01/11–01/11–344-Red, pp. 84–85.

[32]   "Libya Trial: Qaddafi Son Sentenced to Death over War Crimes," BBC News, July 28, 2015.

[33]   *The Prosecutor v. Gaddafi and Al-Senussi*, Decision on the Admissibility of the Case Against Saif Al-Islam Gaddafi, p. 151.

[34]   Ibid.

[35]   For a detailed discussion on fair trial standards in the case *The State of Libya v. Saif al-Islam Qaddafi, Abdullah al-Senussi and Others*, see M. S. Ellis, "Trial of the Libyan regime – An investigation into international fair trial standards," International Bar Association, November 30, 2015.

[36]   Ellis, *Sovereignty and Justice*, p. 221.

[37]   For a longer version of this section, see M. Kersten, "Between Justice and Politics: The International Criminal Court's Intervention in Libya" in C. Stahn, C. De Vos and S. Kendall (eds.), *International*

states in negotiating the demands of diplomacy and justice. Prior to 2011, few could have predicted that international bodies – whether the UN, NATO, or the ICC – would intervene in Libya. As Alex Bellamy observes, no crisis or conflict monitoring group placed Libya at risk of state collapse or descent into civil conflict.[38] In 2010, the country ranked 111th on the "Failed States Index," that is, more stable than countries such as India, Turkey, Russia, and Mexico.[39] While Gaddafi had been seen as a pariah for his sponsorship of, and involvement in, terrorist activities in the 1970s and 1980s, since the early 2000s, the regime had been seen as politically rehabilitated.[40]

By March 2011, however, Libya was mired in civil war, and the deteriorating situation attracted a broad consensus that a coercive international response – including a referral of Libya to the ICC – was warranted. Yet, the unanimous adoption of Resolution 1970 should not be read as reflecting a normative commitment to international justice that had not existed in previous cases. The explicit calls for intervention by the Libyan NTC served to legitimize international action against the Gaddafi regime. Perhaps more importantly, veto-holding members of the P-5, namely Russia and China, did not have vital strategic relationships with Libya as they did with Sudan.[41] Still, a closer examination reveals that some member states on the Security Council were concerned about the potential effects of an ICC intervention. Even with the unanimous referral, statements by Security Council members revealed a degree of caution. For example, in the wake of Resolution 1970, the Chinese and Russian ambassadors to the Security Council avoided any mention of the ICC in explaining their decisions to support the Resolution. Nor did they directly criticize Gaddafi or his government. China explained that the resolution only passed due to "special circumstances," while Russia highlighted that it "opposed counterproductive interventions."[42] India's ambassador suggested that he would have "preferred a 'calibrated approach' to the issue," suggesting the state likewise retained concerns about the role of the ICC.[43]

Criminal Justice and "Local Ownership": Assessing the Impact of Justice Interventions (Cambridge: Cambridge University Press, 2014).

[38] A. J. Bellamy, "Libya and the Responsibility to Protect: The Exception and the Norm" (2011), 25 *Ethics and International Affairs*, 3, p. 4.

[39] "The Failed States Index 2011," *Foreign Policy*, June 14, 2011.

[40] Notably, Qaddafi acknowledged state responsibility for the 1988 bombing of Pan Am flight 103 in which 270 people were killed. Relations between the USA, the UK, and Libya began to thaw in 1999 when Qaddafi handed over to a special court two Libyan nationals accused in the bombing. In exchange, international sanctions were lifted, and Libya ended efforts to obtain nuclear weapons. Libya was subsequently seen as a key Western ally in the global war on terror, providing both intelligence and economic resources. See R. B. St John, *Libya – From Colony to Revolution* (Oxford: Oneworld, 2011); D. Vandewalle, *A History of Modern Libya*, Second Edition (Cambridge:Cambridge University Press, 2012).

[41] A. F. Triponel and P. R. Williams, "The Clash of the Titans: Justice and Realpolitik in Libya" (2012), 28 *American University International Law Review*, 801.

[42] See "In Swift, Decisive Action."   [43]   Ibid.

Moreover, the text of the resolution itself exposed tensions in the aims of the UN Security Council and the Court. In particular, the referral laid bare the uneasy relations between the Council's political interests and the supposed apolitical justice represented by the Court.

Four aspects of Resolution 1970 highlight the politicization of the ICC's mandate by the Security Council: (1) the exclusion of non-state parties (other than Libya) from the jurisdiction of the Court; (2) the inclusion of a reference to Article 16 of the Rome Statute; (3) the temporal limitations imposed on the ICC's jurisdiction in the Libyan case; and (4) the Security Council's prohibition against earmarking any UN funding for the ICC's intervention in Libya. Each will be considered in turn.

First, as with the referral of Darfur to the ICC under Resolution 1593 (2005), Resolution 1970 prohibits the Court from investigating or prosecuting citizens of states that are not party to the Rome Statute "unless such exclusive jurisdiction [of that State] has been waived by the State."[44] Operative paragraph 6 of the Resolution 1970 reads:

[The Security Council] ... [d]ecides that nationals, current or former officials or personnel from a State outside the Libyan Arab Jamahiriya which is not a party to the Rome Statute of the International Criminal Court shall be subject to the exclusive jurisdiction of that State for all alleged acts or omissions arising out of or related to operations in the Libyan Arab Jamahiriya established or authorized by the Council, unless such exclusive jurisdiction has been expressly waived by the State.[45]

The exclusion of non-states parties was done in order to satisfy the United States, which insisted that Operative paragraph 6 be included in the referral as a pre-condition for supporting the resolution.[46] Some have noted the irony of "the United States putting forward a resolution to the Security Council in support of a referral to a court from which it had insisted its military personnel and political elite were immune."[47] Others have criticized the exclusion of citizens of non-states parties because it "fails to respect the Prosecutor's independence and makes it difficult to reconcile the resolution with the principle of equality before the law."[48] More broadly, the exclusion of non-states parties would seem to undermine the Court's aim of achieving universal jurisdiction. However, the mission of Brazil to the United Nations was alone in expressing this specific reservation about expanding the Court's jurisdiction in Libya.[49]

---

[44] For a deeper discussion on the complementarity principle vis-à-vis the Gaddafi case, see Chapter V in Ellis, *Sovereignty and Justice.*

[45] See Security Council Res. 1970.

[46] See du Plessis and Louw, "Justice and the Libyan Crisis," p. 2.

[47] T. Dunne and J. Gifkins, "Libya and the State of Intervention" (2011) 65 *Australian Journal of International Affairs,* 5, p. 525.

[48] R. Cryer, "Sudan, Resolution 1593 and International Criminal Justice" (2006) 19 *Leiden Journal of International Law,* p. 217.

[49] See Security Council Res. 1970.

A second controversial feature of the referral was the inclusion of a preambular reference "recalling article 16 of the Rome Statute under which no investigation or prosecution may be commenced or proceeded with by the International Criminal Court for a period of 12 months after a Security Council request to that effect."[50]

Article 16 of the Rome Statute can be invoked by the UN Security Council to suspend an investigation or prosecution by the Court for up to twelve months, renewable yearly, if the Court's work is found to pose a threat to international peace and security.[51] The reference to Article 16 was included in the referral of Libya to the ICC as a result of some states' concerns that the ICC would complicate the negotiation of a political settlement of the Libyan conflict.[52]

While the inclusion of Article 16 in the Libya referral could be seen as unproblematic given that the article is part of the Rome Statute, numerous proponents of international criminal justice had expected Article 16 would never become salient in practice.[53] For some, the invocation of Article 16 would be contrary to efforts at ending impunity and could allow for manipulation of the ICC's work by the Security Council. The concern and controversy around the Article 16 reference, then, lies both in the possibility that it would calcify a precedent for subsequent case referrals to the ICC, and that it may encourage states to invoke Article 16 as a viable option where political prerogatives – rather than genuine threats to international peace and security – conflict with the aims of justice and accountability. The invocation of Article 16 can, however, be vetoed by any one member of the UNSC.

A third controversial element of Resolution 1970 was the Security Council's restriction on the ICC's temporal jurisdiction. Operative Paragraph 4 of the resolution reads that the Security Council "[d]ecides to refer the situation in the Libyan Arab Jamahiriya since 15 February 2011 to the Prosecutor of the International Criminal Court."[54]

The restriction on the ICC's temporal jurisdiction was controversial in the sense that it limited judicial scrutiny of Western states' support for the Gaddafi regime prior to the Arab Spring. During the post-2003 rehabilitation of the Gaddafi regime from pariah state to strategic ally, many of the same Western states that later intervened in Libya and ensured the regime's collapse had developed strong economic, political, and intelligence connections with the Libyan government. Experts have long held that these relations helped to legitimize the Gaddafi regime.[55] The narrowed timeframe of the referral thus allowed Western states to eschew the question of legal culpability for conditions that, however inadvertently,

---

[50]   Ibid.   [51]   See Rome Statute, Art. 16.

[52]   This is also suggested by Du Plessis and Louw "Justice and the Libyan Crisis," p. 2.

[53]   C. Stahn, "Complementarity, Amnesties and Alternative Forms of Justice: Some Interpretative Guidelines for the International Criminal Court" (2005) 3 *Journal of International Criminal Justice*, 3, pp. 698–699; M. Freeman, *Necessary Evils – Amnesties and the Search for Justice* (Cambridge: Cambridge University Press, 2009).

[54]   Security Council Res. 1970.

[55]   See, for example, St John, *Libya – From Colony to Revolution*, pp. 225–278.

contributed to Gaddafi's violent crackdown. At the same time, the narrow temporal jurisdiction liberated the OTP by focusing its investigation and limiting the scope of incidents that had to be carefully scrutinized.

Finally, Resolution 1970 followed the practice, also established with the referral of Darfur to the ICC under Resolution 1593 (2005), of refusing to provide UN funding for subsequent investigations or prosecutions by the Court. Operative paragraph 8 of Resolution 1970 stated that the Council "[r]ecognizes that none of the expenses incurred in connection with the referral, including expenses related to investigations or prosecutions in connection with that referral, shall be borne by the United Nations and that such costs shall be borne by the parties to the Rome Statute and those States that wish to contribute voluntarily."[56] In effect, the Security Council hamstrung the Office of the Prosecutor before it even began its investigation into the Libyan case.

5.5 DOES JUDICIAL PROCESS UNDERMINE DIPLOMACY?[57]

In the wake of the ICC's intervention and the subsequent issuance of indictments, a diverse array of observers insisted that the Court's intervention would undermine attempts to negotiate a peaceful resolution to the war. Max Boot explained that an ICC warrant left Gaddafi with no incentive but to "fight to the death and take a lot of people down with him."[58] Renowned international lawyer Phillippe Sands, who would later be appointed the Libyan government's legal representative in its admissibility hearings at the ICC, maintained that the ICC "made Gaddafi's orderly, early departure from Libya less likely. Once he was subject to arrest warrants, he was bound to dig in his heels."[59] Scholars Leslie Vinjamuri and Jack Snyder wrote that the ICC was likely to complicate efforts to bring the conflict to an end by leaving the Libyan leader with no way out: "Gaddafi or his core supporters will be unlikely to abdicate power without guarantees against prosecution. The international coalition that backed UN Security Council Resolutions 1970 and 1973 may have boxed itself into a corner."[60] Similarly, the International Crisis Group insisted that the ICC warrant was potentially counter-productive to a negotiated settlement: "[t]o insist that [Gaddafi] both leave the country and face trial in the International Criminal Court is virtually to ensure that he will stay in Libya to the bitter end and go down fighting."[61]

---

[56] Security Council Res. 1970.
[57] This section draws on a longer version of the peace–justice debate in Libya found in Kersten, *Justice in Conflict*.
[58] M. Boot, "Qaddafi Exile Unlikely," Commentary, March 23, 2011.
[59] P. Sands, "The ICC Arrest Warrants Will Make Colonel Qaddafi Dig in His Heels," *The Guardian*, May 4, 2011.
[60] L. Vinjamuri and J. Snyder, "ICC Sheriff Too Quick on the Draw," Duck of Minerva, May 9, 2011.
[61] International Crisis Group, "Popular Protest in North Africa and the Middle East (V): Making Sense of Libya" (June 6, 2011).

However, the empirical record does not support these hypotheses. In fact, the ICC referral did not appear to significantly impact efforts to resolve the conflict. A number of attempts to initiate peace negotiations between the Libyan opposition – including rebel groups – and the Gaddafi regime were undertaken during the civil war. The first came in April 2011, when a high-profile African Union (AU) High-Level Panel, comprised of South African President Jacob Zuma, Mauritanian President Mohamed Ould Abdel Aziz, Malian President Amadou Toumani Toure, Democratic Republic of Congo President Denis Sassou Nguesso and Ugandan President Yoweri Museveni, visited Libya in an attempt to broker an end to hostilities. The AU's proposed peace plan rested on a cessation of hostilities as well as provisions for the unimpeded delivery of humanitarian aid, the protection of foreign nationals, and official peace talks between rebels and the Gaddafi regime aimed at finding a political solution to the crisis.

On April 11, it was announced that Gaddafi had accepted the AU roadmap.[62] However, the Libyan opposition immediately rejected the AU's peace plan. On its visit to Benghazi, then in the hands of opposition rebel factions, slogans like "African Union take Gaddafi with you" greeted the AU delegation. NTC leader Mustafa Abdul Jalil explained that the opposition rejected the AU's peace plan because the "initiative does not include the departure of Gaddafi and his sons from the Libyan political scene, therefore it is outdated."[63] He added: "We will not negotiate with the blood of our martyrs ... We will die with them or be victorious."[64]

As the conflict persisted, Gaddafi began to make overtures, signaling a degree of willingness to negotiate with members of the NATO-led military intervention in Libya (France, the United Kingdom, and the United States). His offers were quickly rejected on the premise that Gaddafi had failed to cease attacks on civilians. Meanwhile, Gaddafi insisted that he was not the official leader of Libya and would not yield power: "I have no official functions to give up – I will not leave my country and will fight to the death."[65] This contradictory position was elaborated in additional comments by the Libyan leader: "We are ready to talk with France and the United States, but with no preconditions. We will not surrender, but I call on you to negotiate. If you want petrol, we will sign contracts with your companies – it is not worth going to war over. Between Libyans, we can solve our problems without being attacked, so pull back your fleets and your planes."[66]

In June, the AU High Level Panel reported that Gaddafi had agreed to remain sidelined in any negotiation process.[67] Still, the opposition demonstrated no interest

---

[62]   "Qaddafi Said to Accept 'Truce Road Map'" Al Jazeera, April 10, 2011.
[63]   See "Libyan Rebels Reject African Union Peace Plan," *The Independent*, April 11, 2011.
[64]   See K. Farim, "Truce Plan for Libya Is Rejected by Rebels," *The New York Times*, April 11, 2011.
[65]   See "Libya: Qaddafi Regime's US–UK Spy Links Revealed," BBC News, September 4, 2011.
[66]   M. Ajhajli and S. Ghasemilee. "NATO, Libyan Rebel Council Reject Qaddafi's Offer for Ceasefire, Negotiations," Al Arabiya News, April 30, 2011.
[67]   See "Qaddafi Vows to 'Stay Out of AU Peace Talks'" Al Jazeera, June 26, 2011.

in negotiating with the regime. NTC Foreign Minister Fathi Baja rejected any negotiations outright: "We refuse completely."[68]

As the conflict dragged on, the international community and the intervening powers hinted at some interest in peace talks. Against the backdrop of concerns amongst intervening powers of a protracted conflict, NATO member states reportedly expressed some anxiety "that the military campaign has not yet succeeded and are keen to explore a political solution."[69] In mid-July, France admitted that indirect negotiations were ongoing with the Gaddafi regime. French defence minister Gérard Longuet even suggested that, in order to satisfy the insistence of the opposition that Gaddafi could not be negotiated with, the Libya leader "will be in another room in his palace with another title."[70] Still, Western powers continued to maintain that Gaddafi had to be removed from power. Longuet, for example, insisted that "[t]he question is not whether he leaves power but how and when."[71]

With the support of at least some Western powers, and in what turned out to be a last-ditch attempt to facilitate dialogue between the Libyan opposition and the regime, in July 2011 Turkey proposed a new, two-stage "roadmap" to bring the civil war to a negotiated conclusion. The Turkish peace plan involved an immediate ceasefire, UN monitoring, the withdrawal of forces loyal to Gaddafi from besieged areas and unimpeded access for humanitarian aid.[72] According to one advisor, Turkey's proposal represented an attempt to "prevent two potential disasters: a protracted civil war in Libya, or partition."[73] It also meant that Gaddafi had to leave office.[74]

At the same time, the African Union requested the "Security Council to activate the provisions of Article 16 of the Rome Statute with a view to deferring the ICC process on Libya, in the interest of Justice as well as peace in the country."[75] However, by that time, the AU had little leverage as a mediator. Moreover, human rights groups voiced concerns in response to any potential deferral of the ICC's intervention. Richard Dicker of Human Rights Watch argued that "diplomats may be thinking of using a possible escape hatch contained in the ICC's treaty . . . . This truly unfortunate provision authorizes political interference in a judicial proceeding, and it should be used only in exceptional circumstances."[76] In the end, there is no evidence the Security Council contemplated invoking Article 16.

Still, Jalil intimated that the NTC had softened its position on Gaddafi by declaring that the Libyan leader could feasibly remain in the country "under

---

[68] "Libya: Zuma Says Qaddafi Will Not Quit," BBC News, May 31, 2011.
[69] I. Black, "Turkey Asks Libya Summit to Back Peace Negotiations," *The Guardian*, July 14, 2011.
[70] See "Qaddafi Regime in Talks with France," Al Jazeera, July 11, 2011.
[71] See J. Lichfield, "France Confirms Negotiations with Qaddafi Regime," *The Independent*, July 12, 2011.
[72] Black, "Turkey Asks Libya Summit to Back Peace Negotiations."
[73] I. Kalin, "A Roadmap for Libya," *The Guardian*, May 12, 2011.   [74] Ibid.
[75] See African Union, "Decisions Adopted During the 17th African Union Summit" (July 1, 2011).
[76] R. Dicker, "Handing Qaddafi a Get-Out-Of-Jail-Free Card," *The New York Times*, August 1, 2011.

international supervision."[77] Attempts to find a solution to the question of Gaddafi's fate were also met by a softening on the part of UK First Secretary of State William Hague who claimed that "[w]hat happens to Gaddafi is ultimately a question for the Libyans." French Foreign Minister Alain Juppé similarly suggested Gaddafi could remain "in Libya on one condition, which I repeat: that he very clearly steps aside from Libyan political life."[78] Such remarks suggested that the international community was willing to provide Gaddafi with a de facto amnesty, allowing the Libyan colonel to escape ICC prosecution.

Human rights groups were wary of any deal that would protect Gaddafi from accountability. Dicker, for example, decried any potential "get-out-of-jail-free card" for the Libyan leader and warned that it would not only hinder the pursuit of justice, but that any "plan that gives Gaddafi a comfortable retirement (inside or outside of Libya) is short-sighted. Gaddafi ... would remain a destabilizing figure."[79] The ICC also weighed in, insisting that Gaddafi had to be arrested and surrendered to the Court.[80]

In the end, as opposition factions began to take over the capital of Tripoli in August 2011, the prospects of a negotiated resolution were overrun by facts on the ground. At that point, the opposition was disinclined to accept a negotiated transition. One NTC official, Guma el-Gamaty stated the opposition has zero interest in negotiating with Gaddafi and that "[t]he only negotiation is how to apprehend him, [for him] to tell us where he is and what conditions he wants for his apprehension: whether he wants to be kept in a single cell or shared cell or whether he wants to have his own shower or not, you know. These are the kind of negotiations we are willing to talk about."[81]

As the above overview suggests, there is no clear evidence that the ICC directly impeded conflict resolution processes in Libya. Some policy makers expressed concern that an arrest warrant would limit the possibility of peace negotiations by restricting Gaddafi's options for leaving the country.[82] Yet, there is no evidence in the public record that Gaddafi explicitly challenged the referral as an obstacle to his participation in peace negotiations.

5.6 INSTRUMENTALIZING THE COURT FOR DIPLOMATIC ENDS

While the ICC referral and subsequent indictments by the Pre-Trial Chamber did not seem directly to fuel conflict dynamics in the way some analysts predicted, the

---

[77]   See R. Norton-Taylor and C. Stephen, "Qaddafi Can't be Left in Libya, Says International Criminal Court," *The Guardian*, July 26, 2011.

[78]   See A. Cowell, "In Shift, Britain Says Qaddafi Could Remain in Libya," *The New York Times*, July 26, 2011.

[79]   Dicker, "Handing Qaddafi a Get-Out-Of-Jail-Free Card."

[80]   See Norton-Taylor and Stephen, "Qaddafi Can't Be Left in Libya."

[81]   See D. Smith, "Qaddafi Offers to Negotiate with Libya Rebels Over Transfer of Power," *The Guardian*, August 28, 2011.

[82]   See B. D. Schaefer, "International Criminal Court Complicates Conflict Resolution in Libya," Heritage Foundation, June 9, 2011.

inherently political nature of the Security Council vis-à-vis the ICC – including the referral process itself, funding constraints imposed by Resolution 1970, and the place of the Prosecutor within that political environment – invariably affected the broader international response to the crisis in Libya.

As a practical matter, the Security Council embodies the interests of its constituent states. To the extent the Security Council decides to refer a situation to the ICC, as it did with Resolution 1970, the interests of member states are embedded in the decision to deploy the tools of international justice.[83] This is not to say that the Security Council can control or even anticipate the response of the OTP; indeed, the UNSC was rather surprised by the quick pace with which the ICC initiated its investigation and issued indictments in the Libyan case. Rather, the political nature of the ICC referral informs the way in which the UNSC responds to and leverages developments at the Court.

Through this lens, the OTP's decision to open an investigation, and the indictments that followed, served to legitimize the international intervention in Libya. The March 3, 2011 announcement by Moreno-Ocampo that a formal investigation would be opened into the crisis "effectively indicated to the international community that he had found a reasonable basis to believe that crimes against humanity had been committed in Libya since February 15."[84] Although not equivalent to a legal finding of fact, this move by the OTP was leveraged by Western leaders as they framed a moral case for intervention.[85] In other words, the ICC's investigation, resulting from the Security Council's referral in Resolution 1970, had the political effect of placing the Court's imprimatur on further intervention, including the use of force under Chapter VII of the UN Charter as authorized by Resolution 1973.

The political dynamic between the UNSC and the Court was further complicated by the advent of the "responsibility to protect" (R2P). Among other tenets of R2P, the norm calls for the international community to take measures to protect vulnerable populations – by force, if necessary – where a state fails to do so or is the perpetrator of crimes.[86] The UN Security Council cited a responsibility to protect citizens in both Resolution 1970 and 1973. Libya was the first case where R2P was explicitly invoked as an animating force for humanitarian intervention.

As Andrea Birdsall notes, the invocation of R2P creates a potentially problematic relationship between the Security Council and the Court. R2P is a "political concept" meant to galvanize international response to urgent humanitarian crises.[87]

---

[83] Triponnel and Williams, "The Clash of the Titans," p. 805.
[84] Ibid., p. 814. See also Rome Statute, Art. 53(1)(a): "In deciding whether to initiate an investigation, the Prosecutor shall consider whether the information available to the Prosecutor provides a reasonable basis to believe that a crime within the jurisdiction of the Court has been or is being committed."
[85] Triponnel and Williams, "The Clash of the Titans," p. 814.
[86] See ICISS, "The Responsibility to Protect" (December 2001).
[87] A. Birdsall, "The Responsibility to Protect and the ICC: A Problematic Relationship?" (2015), 26 *Criminal Law Forum*, 1, p. 55.

The ICC, for its part, is a legal institution, whose legitimacy derives from ostensibly apolitical investigations and prosecutions within a framework of international law. In the case of Libya, the urgency with which international action was demanded in response to R2P may have accelerated the Resolution 1970 referral, thus implicating the ICC in the military intervention – and, ultimately, the regime change – that followed.

Inasmuch as regime change was not the stated goal of Resolution 1973, the NATO-led intervention is generally seen as an excess that "overstretched" the concept of R2P to its detriment.[88] This is not to argue that the Security Council was improper in recognizing a legitimate political, legal, and humanitarian interest in referring Libya to the ICC. Rather, the urgency instigated by invoking R2P may have foreclosed possibilities of strategic, deliberate coordination between the UNSC and the ICC such that the institutional aims of the latter became conflated with the former.

5.7 CONCLUSION

As one scholar has observed, the project of international justice often complicates the project of conflict resolution.[89] Conversely, the practices and procedures of the International Criminal Court, as a primary tool of international justice, are often complicated by the diplomatic priorities and power politics of the UN Security Council. What does the case of Libya reveal about the prospect of reconciling these often competing claims of law and diplomacy?

The inherently political nature of the Security Council means that any referral to the ICC will necessarily reflect the interests of member states and the geopolitical environment in which the referral is made. In the case of Libya, the legitimizing claims of the NTC, as well as the lack of strategic ties to Libya by members of the P-5, were permissive for the Security Council's referral. However, the limitations on ICC funding and temporal jurisdiction included in Resolution 1970 reflect the ex ante constraints imposed on the Court and the OTP, belying the notion of a fully autonomous mechanism of international justice. At the same time, the swift response by the OTP in initiating its investigation and obtaining indictments afforded legitimacy and political cover to international intervention by underscoring the perceived criminality of the Gaddafi regime. This intervention, in turn, resulted in regime change and the death of Gaddafi at the hands of rebel forces beyond the reach of international judicial processes.

This case study does not suggest that the UN Security Council referral to the ICC was a strategic act to legitimize international intervention and regime change. Such outcomes could not have been foreseen with certainty. However, it is precisely the uncertainty of outcomes in conflict situations, accentuated by the urgency of

---

[88]   Ibid.   [89]   See Kersten, *Justice in Conflict*.

invoking R2P, that calls for deeper understanding of the dynamics between diplomatic and judicial actors.

The ICC was hamstrung from the outset of its investigation in Libya, and its ability to promote justice in this case has been compromised. Some argue the Court's intervention served as a moral stamp of approval for opposition groups, which did not face indictments. By this account, the indictment of Muammar Gaddafi applied an international imprimatur to his deposition and further undermined any incentives to pursue a negotiated settlement to the conflict.[90] Moreover, the OTP's decision not to pursue arrest warrants for opposition or rebel leaders compounded the perception of one-sided accountability already entrenched in Libya by the National Transitional Council. Notably, the NTC passed an amnesty law in May 2012 shielding any "military, security or civil actions dictated by the February 17 Revolution that were performed by revolutionaries with the goal of promoting or protecting the revolution."[91] The OTP's decision to forgo investigating opposition figures protected rebel and militia factions from criminal accountability and could be seen as contributing to a culture of impunity in post-war Libya.

In the cases where the OTP did seek indictments, an adherence to the principle of complementarity may have come at the expense of full access to justice. While the Rome Statute is premised on complementarity, the Libya case reflects the complexity of balancing deference to domestic courts and the demands of international standards. Responding to admissibility challenges, the Pre-Trial Chamber made decisions about the willingness and ability of the Libyan government to adequately investigate the charges against Gadaffi and Senussi. But once the initial decision about admissibility was made, the Court and the OTP did not continue to review the implementation of judicial proceedings on the ground. The Libya case exemplifies the challenges for both the Court and the OTP of determining how complementarity applies in practice, as well as its implications for whether the obligations of international justice are truly met.

Conversely, some have argued that the ICC has in fact been effective in shaping post-conflict justice in Libya. Former Chief Prosecutor of the ICC Luis Moreno-Ocampo remarked that, while the situation in Libya is complex and increasingly precarious, the arrest of Saif al-Islam and Abdullah al-Senussi indicates that Libya was "a successful story in terms of stopping the crimes . . . I think it is still providing an important service, because we will ensure justice in Libya, whoever will do it."[92] Moreno-Ocampo seems to suggest the pressure of ICC scrutiny has compelled the Libyan government to fulfill its international legal obligations in line with the principle of positive complementarity.

---

[90] See also M. Kersten, "The ICC and Its Impact: More Known Unknowns," Open Democracy, November 4, 2014.

[91] See Human Rights Watch, "Libya: Amend New Special Procedures" (May 11, 2012).

[92] T. Papenfuss, "Interview with Luis Moreno-Ocampo, Chief Prosecutor of the International Criminal Court," IPI Global Observatory, January 25, 2012.

Following the end of the conflict, the ICC has seen interest in its mandate in Libya gradually erode. The support of the international community for the ICC, signaled by the unanimous referral of the situation in Libya to the Court, began to dissipate during the later stages of the war as states declared that the fate of Gaddafi lay in the hands of Libyans and not with the Court. US Ambassador to the UN Susan Rice, for example, declared that the fate of Gaddafi was "something that must be decided not by the United States or any other government, but by the people of Libya and by the interim transitional government that we expect will soon be constituted ... These are all choices that the Libyan people will ultimately have to make for them."[93]

Against this backdrop of waning international interest, the situation in Libya has continued to deteriorate. The country has been described as "lawless."[94] Human rights advocates have been assassinated, torture and arbitrary detention by various militias has been well documented. According to the International Crisis Group, Libya's "trial by error" approach to post-conflict justice has triggered "more grievances, further undermining confidence in the state."[95] Peace negotiations between two factions (one in Tripoli, the other Tobruk) purporting to be the official government of Libya are ongoing. But post-conflict state-building has been painfully slow and has been undermined by the continued political prominence of militias and criminal networks. As one leading observer says, "Libyans used to be afraid of a brutal state; now they are afraid of the absence of the state."[96]

BIBLIOGRAPHY

Primary Sources

African Union, "Decisions Adopted During the 17th African Union Summit" (July 1, 2011).
The Prosecutor v. Saif Al-Islam Gaddafi and Abdullah Al-Senussi, Application on Behalf of the Government of Libya Pursuant to Article 19 of the ICC Statute [2012] ICC-01/11–01/11.
The Prosecutor v. Saif Al-Islam Gaddafi and Abdullah Al-Senussi, Decision on the Admissibility of the Case Against Abdullah Al-Senussi [2013] ICC-01/11–01/11.
The Prosecutor v. Saifal-Islam Gaddafi and Abdullah Al-Senussi, Decision on the Admissibility of the Case Against Saif Al-Islam Gaddafi [2013] ICC-01/11–01/11–344-Red.
Rome Statute of the International Criminal Court, Rome, July 17, 1998, in force July 1, 2002, 2187 UNTS 38544.

---

93   See C. Lynch, "Rice Says Libyan People Can Decide Whether to try Qaddafi; ICC Says Not So Fast," *Foreign Policy*, August 23, 2011.
94   F. Chothia, "Why Is Libya Lawless?" BBC News, January 27, 2015.
95   International Crisis Group, "Trial by Error: Justice in Post-Qadhafi Libya" (April 17, 2013).
96   To learn more about state-building and criminal networks, see: M. Shaw and F. Mangan, "Illicit Trafficking and Libya's Transition: Profits and Losses," United States Institute of Peace, February 24, 2014. For more commentary from the observer, see H. Matar, "The Killing of Abdelsalam al-Mismari, and the Triumph of Fear in Libya," *The Guardian*, July 30, 2013.

Situation in the Libyan Arab Jamahiriya, Prosecutor's Application Pursuant to Article 58 as to Muammar Mohammed Abu Minyar Gadadfi, Saif Al-Islam Gaddafi and Abdullah Al-Senussi [2011] ICC-01/11.

Situation in The Libyan Arab Jamahiriya, Warrant of Arrest for Abdullah Al-Senussi [2011] ICC-01/11–15.

Situation in The Libyan Arab Jamahiriya, Warrant of Arrest for Muammar Mohammed Abu Minyar Gadaffi [2011] ICC-01/11–13.

Situation in The Libyan Arab Jamahiriya, Warrant of Arrest for Saif Al-Islam Gaddafi [2011] ICC-01/11–14.

United Nations Human Rights Council, "Report of the International Commission of Inquiry on Libya" (March 2, 2012) UN Doc. A/HRC/19/68.

United Nations Press Release, "In Swift, Decisive Action, Security Council Imposes Tough Measures on Libyan Regime, Adopting Resolution 1970 in Wake of Crackdown on Protesters," February 26, 2011.

United Nations Security Council (UNSC), Resolution 1970 (February 26, 2011) UN Doc. S/RES/1970.

UNSC, Resolution 1973 (March 17, 2011), UN Doc. S/RES/1973.

Secondary Sources

Books

Ellis M., *Sovereignty and Justice: Balancing the Principle of Complementarity between International and Domestic War Crimes Tribunals* (Cambridge: Cambridge Scholars Publishing, 2014).

Freeman M., *Necessary Evils – Amnesties and the Search for Justice* (Cambridge: Cambridge University Press, 2009).

St John R. B., *Libya: From Colony to Revolution* (London: Oneworld, 2011)

Kersten M., "Between Justice and Politics: The International Criminal Court's Intervention in Libya" in Stahn C., De Vos C. and Kendall S. (eds.), *International Criminal Justice and "Local Ownership": Assessing the Impact of Justice Interventions* (Cambridge: Cambridge University Press, 2014).

Kersten M., *Justice in Conflict: The Effects of the International Criminal Court's Interventions on Ending Wars and Building Peace* (Oxford: Oxford University Press, 2016).

Schabas W., *An Introduction to the International Criminal Court* (Cambridge: Cambridge University Press, 2007).

Scheffer D., *All the Missing Souls: A Personal History of the War Crimes Tribunals* (Princeton: Princeton University Press, 2011).

Vandewalle D., *A History of Modern Libya*, Second Edition (Cambridge: Cambridge University Press, 2012).

Articles and Reports

Ajbaili M. and Ghasemilee S., "NATO, Libyan Rebel Council Reject Gaddafi's Offer for Ceasefire, Negotiations," Al Arabiya News, April 30, 2011.

Bellamy, A. J., "Libya and the Responsibility to Protect: The Exception and the Norm" (2011) 25 *Ethics & International Affairs*, 3, pp. 263–269.

Birdsall A., "The Responsibility to Protect and the ICC: A Problematic Relationship?" (2015) 26 *Criminal Law Forum*, 1, pp. 51–72.

Black I., "Turkey Asks Libya Summit to Back Peace Negotiations," *The Guardian*, July 14, 2011.

Boot M., "Gaddafi Exile Unlikely," *Commentary Magazine*, March 23, 2011.

Chesterman S., "Leading from Behind': The Responsibility to Protect, The Obama Doctrine, and Humanitarian Intervention After Libya" (2011) 25 *Ethics & International Affairs*, 3, pp. 11–35.

Chothia F., "Why Is Libya Lawless?" BBC News, January 27, 2015.

Cowell A., "In Shift, Britain Says Gaddafi Could Remain in Libya," *The New York Times*, July 26, 2011.

Cryer R., "Sudan, Resolution 1593 and International Criminal Justice" (2006) 19 *Leiden Journal of International Law*, 1, pp. 195–222.

Dicker R., "Handing Gaddafi a Get-Out-Of-Jail-Free Card," *The New York Times*, August 1, 2011.

Du Plessis M. and Louw A., "Justice and the Libyan Crisis: The ICC's Role under Security Council Resolution 1970," ISS Briefing Paper, May 31, 2011.

Dunne T. and Gifkins J., "Libya and the State of Intervention" (2011) 65 *Australian Journal of International Affairs*, 5, 515–529.

Ellis M., "Trial of the Libyan Regime – An Investigation into International Fair Trial Standards," International Bar Association, November 2015.

Ellis M., "Peace for All or Justice for One?" *The New York Times*, August 12, 2011.

Kareen F., "Truce Plan for Libya Is Rejected by Rebels," *The New York Times*, April 11, 2011.

"The Failed States Index 2011," *Foreign Policy*, June 14, 2011.

"Gaddafi's Death May Be War Crime: ICC Prosecutor," Reuters, December 16, 2011.

"Gaddafi Regime in Talks with France," Al Jazeera, July 10, 2011.

"Gaddafi Said to Accept Truce Road Map," Al Jazeera, April 10, 2011.

"Gaddafi Vows to Stay Out of AU Peace Talks," Al Jazeera, June 26, 2011.

Goldstone R., "ICC's Libyan Crisis Shows Saif Gaddafi Should Be Tried in The Hague," *The Guardian*, June 22, 2012.

Heller K. J., "The International Commission of Inquiry on Libya: A Critical Analysis" in Meierhenrich J. (ed.), *International Commissions: The Role of Commissions of Inquiry in the Investigation of International Crimes* 2013. Available at: http://ssrn.com/abstract=2123782.

Human Rights Watch, "Libya: Amend New Special Procedures," May 11, 2012.

International Crisis Group (ICG), "Popular Protest in North Africa and the Middle East (V): Making Sense of Libya" (June 6, 2011).

ICG, "Trial by Error: Justice in Post-Qadhafi Libya" (April 17, 2013).

Kalin I., "A Roadmap for Libya," *The Guardian*, May 12, 2011.

Kersten M., "The ICC and Its Impact: More Known Unknowns," Open Democracy, November 4, 2014.

"Libya Commander Abdel Hakim Belhaj to Sue UK Government," BBC News, December 19, 2011.

"Libya: Gaddafi Regime's US-UK Spy Links Revealed," BBC News, September 4, 2011.

"Libya Protests: Defiant Gaddafi Refuses to Quit," BBC News, February 22, 2011.

"Libyan Rebels Reject African Union Peace Plan," *The Independent*, April 11, 2011.

"Libya: Zuma Says Gaddafi Will Not Quit," BBC News, May 31, 2011.

Lichfield J., "France Confirms Negotiations with Gaddafi Regime," *The Independent*, July 12, 2011.

Lynch C., "Rice Says Libyan People Can Decide Whether to Try Gaddafi; ICC Says Not So Fast," *Foreign Policy*, August 23, 2011.

Matar H., "The Killing of Abdelsalam al-Mismari, and the Triumph of Fear in Libya," *The Guardian*, July 30, 2013.

Norton-Taylor R. and Stephen C., "Gaddafi Can't Be Left in Libya, Says International Criminal Court," *The Guardian*, July 26, 2011.

Philippe S., "The ICC Arrest Warrants Will Make Colonel Gaddafi Dig in His Heels" *The Guardian*, May 4, 2011.

Shaw M. and Mangan F., "Illicit Trafficking and Libya's Transition: Profits and Losses," United States Institute for Peace, February 24, 2014.

Smith D., "Gaddafi Offers to Negotiate with Libya Rebels Over Transfer of Power," *The Guardian,* August 28, 2011.

Stahn C., "Complementarity, Amnesties and Alternative Forms of Justice: Some Interpretative Guidelines for the International Criminal Court" (2005) 3 *Journal of International Criminal Justice*, 3, pp. 695–720.

Triponel, Anna F. and Williams, Paul R. "The Clash of the Titans: Justice and Realpolitik in Libya" (2012) 28 *American University Journal of International Law*, pp. 775–834.

Vinjamuri L. and Snyder J., "ICC Sheriff Too Quick on the Draw" Duck of Minerva, May 9, 2011.

"What Gaddafi Said," *Foreign Affairs*, June 4, 2011.

Conclusion

The relationship between law and diplomacy is complex and rife with contradiction, including, as illustrated in the case studies in this book, occasional collisions between judicial and diplomatic processes. The International Criminal Court (ICC) and international tribunals function in a political world and cannot be blind to the political consequences of legal proceedings. At the same time, diplomats seeking to resolve and negotiate conflicts may find themselves restricted by the emerging frameworks and mechanisms of international humanitarian law. The parameters for bartering peace against justice have tightened. Impunity no longer has a place in the diplomatic toolbox.

Nevertheless, there remains a degree of flexibility within international law for diplomats who understand the nature and nuance of judicial processes and for prosecutors who are aware of the political background of crisis situations. As illustrated by several of the case studies presented in this book, the enforcement of international criminal law is conditioned on the robust and complementary application of both law and diplomacy, which in turn requires state cooperation in the implementation of criminal tribunal decisions. At the same time, any attempt to look for alignments between judicial and diplomatic processes is fraught with complexities. Fortuitous alignments, as in the case of Bosnia, can serve negotiations to end conflict and war, and ultimately contribute to the effective implementation of international and transitional justice. Not all cases can be resolved in such a fashion. In any case, the independence of the judiciary that should not be politicized must be preserved, both in practice and in public perception.

On the other hand, there can be contradictions in these parallel processes, as illustrated by the case of Libya, where the pursuit of justice was seen as complicating, or even hampering, the goal of conflict resolution. The case of Darfur further illustrates how two separate, but interconnected processes – namely an ICC investigation and the parallel diplomatic effort to end the conflict and achieve South Sudan's independence – can be mutually constraining. The international community as a whole clearly sent Khartoum mixed signals, and in so doing failed to devise and uphold a strategy for Darfur that was coherent and consistent over time. As a result, the Sudanese army and Janjaweed militias continued in the perpetration of mass atrocities. The case studies raise questions about what can be done to better align the timing of judicial and diplomatic efforts, and to manage a signaling strategy to minimize the negative effects that judicial actions can have on state behavior.

Advisors might help courts or tribunals decode the diplomatic landscape and help the prosecutor better understand the political dynamics surrounding judicial decisions, but the independence of the judiciary, as noted, must be guaranteed both in perception and reality. Experience shows that prosecutors use their discretion not only regarding the timing of an indictment but also whether or not it is sealed, and whether they start with "low-level" indictees or those further up the chain of command.

When states support accountability on the domestic level and, through diplomatic pressure cooperate with other states on the international level, accountability will override impunity. The Kosovo study illustrated that it took both internal and external political pressure to achieve Milošević's transfer to The Hague. But the opposite is also true – accountability through international law is all but impossible without the political will of states and the international community. As highlighted in the Darfur case, the UN Security Council has been completely impotent in enforcing the ICC's indictment against President Al-Bashir, even though the Security Council referred the Darfur Situation to the Court in the first place. In the face of catastrophic conflict, diplomatic interests do not always align with international criminal law, and accountability, if deemed impractical, is quickly jettisoned.

As depicted by some of the case studies presented in this book, the enforcement of international criminal law is conditioned on the effective operation of diplomatic and legal processes. The Kosovo case study highlights how tactical diplomacy can assist in carrying out international arrest warrants, just as it raises important questions about whether and how cooperation between judicial and political actors can serve to promote shared goals in ending violence without undermining the integrity of international justice.

The Bosnian case study illustrates the potential of international criminal indictments to support conflict resolution, demonstrating how existing indictments can be leveraged to move and "unclog" the diplomatic process, offering advantages at the negotiating table. In contrast, in the Darfur case where the degree of cooperation between ICC and concerned states has been minimal, the judicial process is stalled, some African Union Rome Statute signatories are criticizing ICC, and the peace process is deadlocked.

One early example of aligning judicial and diplomatic processes occurred at the ICTY. Independent political advisors were seconded to the Tribunal to assist the Office of the Prosecutor. Their function was to help decode the diplomatic landscape and provide the Prosecutor with a better understanding of the political dynamics surrounding the cases at hand. The ICC has followed this example by employing, rather than seconding, political advisors to the prosecutor.

There remains a question as to the degree of effort that should go into cultivating such cooperation. For instance, if alignment can be achieved by design, how would the international community ensure that it does not lead to politicized judicial decisions, or have an adverse effect on diplomatic efforts aimed at conflict resolution? In the end, a prosecutor will undoubtedly be judged fairly or unfairly by the timing of his or her indictment, and by the impartial exercise of his or her responsibilities. The Rwandan case illustrates a further complication of joint or parallel diplomatic and judicial efforts, namely how confusion over legal terms can hinder the international community's effective response to humanitarian crises and conflict. The Rwandan example underscores the importance of the proper use of legal terminology in diplomacy.

For example, use of the term "genocide" in UN Security Council Resolution 912 and subsequent resolutions led to protracted deliberations and debates among diplomats and members of the Security Council in the midst of escalating violence in Rwanda. The debate was borne out of uncertainty, confusion and misunderstanding in relation to the legal implications of the term in official resolutions and statements. In particular, a number of states were hesitant to refer to the violence as "genocide" for fear of triggering a legal duty to intervene under the Genocide Convention. This preoccupation with describing the killings as "genocide" complicated the diplomatic discussions about how to end the violence in Rwanda. Lack of clarity surrounding legal terminology can be used as an excuse by states to abandon their responsibilities under the pretext of legal uncertainty.

International humanitarian law and its enforcement mechanisms have expanded significantly since the first ad hoc war crimes tribunals for the former Yugoslavia and Rwanda in the 1990s. There have been additional ad hoc tribunals, most prominently those for Lebanon and Sierra Leone, as well as hybrid tribunals such as the special tribunal for Cambodia and, of course, the permanent International Criminal Court in The Hague established in 2002. As of March 2016, 124 states have ratified the Rome Statute binding themselves to compliance with the ICC, with an additional thirty-one signatory states pending ratification. The forty-two that have not signed include China (a permanent member of the UNSC), India, and Indonesia. The United States and Russia, also P5 members, are both signatories but have not ratified the Rome Statute.

While the reach of international humanitarian justice has expanded significantly over the past three decades, the principles and dynamics underlying judicial and diplomatic processes have remained essentially unchanged. It is hoped that the case studies contained in this book can provide guidance and insight for diplomats and jurists alike in the advancement of peace through accountability and the rule of law.

Index